YOU
Make a Difference

50 Heart-Centered Entrepreneurs Share Their Stories of Inspiration and Transformation

Created by
Babypie Publishing Company

Book Cover Design by Cathi Stevenson
www.BookCoverExpress.com

Interior Design by Rudy Milanovich
rudy@wizardvision.net

Interviews by
"The Book Guy" Keith Leon
www.TheyCallMeTheBookGuy.com
www.BakeYourBook.com

Transcriptions by
Jess Steinman
www.InTouchWithSpirit.com

Book Edited by
Jess Steinman – www.InTouchWithSpirit.com
Heather Marsh – www.ClassicEditing.com
Maura Leon – www.MauraLeon.com

ISBN: 978-0-9884471-0-3

Babypie Publishing Company
Waitsfield, Vermont

Dedication

This book is dedicated to heart-centered entrepreneurs everywhere who are following their passions and making a difference. Because of their efforts, this world is a better place.

Contents

Success Training

Health & Wellness

Arts & Education

Business Support

Spiritual Development

Acknowledgements

For their support in bringing this book to fruition, we would like to thank our team of angels, including:

Heather Reinhardt, Uriel, Janet Bray Attwood, Lissa Coffey, Barbara De Angelis, Ariel, Marjean Holden, Dr. Bob Levine, Michael, Adam Markel, Peak Potentials Training, Charles Poliquin, Gabriel, Dr. Joe Rubino, Marcia Wieder, Maribel Jimenez, Insight Seminars, Jared Allardyce, Rudy Milanovich, Metatron, Jess Steinman, Andrew Zirkin, Raphael, Heather Marsh, Cathi Stevenson, Agape International Spiritual Center, and all our patient, loving, and understanding family members.

Introduction

One sunny spring day while we were enjoying the beauty of nature by a lake, a question arose: "How can we share with the world all of the incredible, heart-centered entrepreneurs we have been so blessed to connect with over the years?" Once the question was out, the answer came quickly and easily and, being the doers that we are, we acted swiftly to implement the resulting plan.

This book is the answer to that question, the result of those actions, and the product of that plan. We have contacted and interviewed all of the truly authentic, heart-centered business owners we know. All of these people are doing what they do because they are passionate about being of service to humanity.

We invite you to read all of these stories with an open heart and an open mind. These business owners are going to be vulnerable, open, honest, and will share their hearts with you. As you read their answers to the illuminating five questions we asked each participant, you'll get to know them and when you find a need for the service they offer, you'll have their contact information right here in this book. When it comes time for you to call them and do business, all you need do is walk over, open the book, and contact them.

Happy reading!

Maura and Keith Leon
Babypie Publishing Company

Success Training

Janet Bray Attwood

"Whenever you're faced with a choice, decision, or an opportunity, choose in favor of your passions,"

Janet Bray Attwood, is the *New York Times* best-selling co-author of *The Passion Test: The Effortless Path to Discovering Your Life Purpose*. The Passion Test is presently the number one tool being used around the world to align people with their passions.

Janet has presented her programs on the same stage with the Dalai Lama, Sir Richard Branson, Stephen Covey, Jack Canfield, Lisa Nichols, and many others.

Janet has taken hundreds of thousands of people through The Passion Test process, all over the world. She is the founder of The Passion Test Certification Program, which presently has over 1000 Certified Facilitators in over 48 countries. Janet is also the founder of The Passion Test for Business, The Passion Test for Kids & Teens, The Passion Test for Kids in Lockdown, and The Passion Test: Reclaim Your Power Program for the homeless.

Janet received the *President's Volunteer Service Award* from the President of the United States, the highest award for recognition of volunteer service in the U.S.

To find out more: www.ThePassionTest.com

What personal event or universal problem made you want to do what you do?

Like many people, I was once in a job that I felt I was failing at, miserably, and it was a horrible feeling! I was recruiting disk-drive engineers in Silicon Valley. My friends had offered me the job. They said, "Janet, you'll be recruiting disk-drive engineers and it will be fun! You'll get to work with all your buddies, and we're making millions of dollars! You're so good at communicating and so vivacious and enthusiastic, it will be a no-brainer for you!"

The only thing I heard was that I would make millions of dollars; you could see dollar bill signs popping out of my eyes! I was teaching meditation, in Palo Alto, California, at the time that I got this job offer. I loved teaching transcendental meditation; it was a total blast. I loved talking about spirituality and hanging out with spiritual people. This was over 20 years ago, and the downside was that I was, literally, sleeping on the transcendental meditation center floor at the time. Every morning when I wanted to take a shower, there wasn't a shower in the office, so I would sneak across the street, hop over the fence, and sneak into this local apartment building's pool shower to take my shower. Then I would run back across the street and give my enlightened seminars. So when I got this job offer, I thought: *Yay! I'll actually have my own shower and more than a couple of dresses!*

I went to this job and they had a bell, in the recruiting office, which they rang every single day when they got a job for a recruiter. It was at the front of the room, and they'd run up to the front every time they got a recruiter, and this bell was ringing all day long, for *everybody*, except for—guess who—Little Janet Attwood. I was dying, because at the time I didn't know myself well enough to know that *I* wasn't my job. Who I was, *was* my job, and to fail at it, miserably, was really deplorable for me in all areas. My ego was totally thrashed. I'd hear, *"Ring! Ring! Ring!"* and I'd sit there, slumping down, day after day, farther in my seat and getting more depressed. Every day, after work, I would go and meditate. One such day, when I came out of meditation, I saw this sign on the wall that said, "Yes to Success™ Seminars—Success Seminar in San Francisco." I'd been praying for a sign to get me out of my Hell, because I was really in Hell, being so terrible at this job. Terrible is really a soft word; I totally sucked at this job.

My mom always said, "Janet, you're here for some greatness! You're my little angel and I know you're here to do great things."

I started putting my attention on *what* and asked, "Please, God, help!" I was drowning in my misery. When I saw this sign on the wall, I said, "That's it! That sign is *the* sign!" So, the next day I called in sick to work, drove to San Francisco, and plopped myself down in the front seat of this seminar. This woman comes on, and she was completely on fire! She was talking about being in your integrity, doing the things you love, choosing in favor of what you care most about, and that the way to power is to really know who you are. As she was talking, I felt like I was 100 feet off the ground! She was speaking right to me. There were people in the room, but it was all coming at me. That was a really neat experience because, as I was watching her, I realized I had an "aha" moment. I wanted to be just like her! I wanted to *be* her, *do* what she was doing…and she had to be my mentor.

The second big thing that happened was that she talked about a survey that had been given to the 100 most successful people in the United States. The survey found that the 100 most successful people were *all* living their top five passions. When she said that, it was like someone hit me over the head. "That's it! If I can figure out what my top five passions are, then I'll be like those 100 most successful people in the United States!"

So, sucking in that job was the personal event *and* my universal problem that made me want to find out what I really wanted to do. In that moment, I started to download what is now known all over the world as the number one tool to help people discover and live their passions— The Passion Test. We were recently featured in *O Magazine* in their cover story called, "Find Your Calling."

What has been the hardest part of doing what you do?

The hardest part has been consistently choosing in favor of my passions. In *The Passion Test*, we talk about the secret to living a passionate life. The secret is whenever you're faced with a choice, a decision, or an opportunity, choose in favor of your passions. I ended up mentoring with the woman who presented the seminar in San Francisco and was on my way to becoming a "transformational leader." Then I met a guy, fell in love, and we eloped. The next thing I knew, two weeks into the marriage, his ex-wife called up and told my new husband that she couldn't handle having the kids because she needed her own time, and that he had to now come pick them up. All of a sudden—boom!—instant mom. I had a one-and-a-half-year-old and a three-year-old, and I'd only been married two weeks.

When we say, "Whenever you're faced with a choice, decision, or an opportunity, choose in favor of your passions," it doesn't always mean it's going to be easy. I chose in favor of the children. There I was, on the way out to do the job I had longed for, studied for, and practiced for, when these little kids came along and everything shifted. I could feel their little hearts were so in need of massive amounts of love. What I forgot to choose in favor of, along with them, was *me*; I gave up all of my other passions for them. And I'm not the only one who does this! As I've traveled around the world, for the last ten years, giving The Passion Test, I've seen this as a universal "plague"—choosing in favor of what other people want you to do, or what you think you should do. We "should" all over ourselves, all the time, and forget about ourselves. It's hard not to. In my example, I had these two little kids, who suddenly didn't have their mom, and their dad was working all the time. What do you do? Of course, you take care of them. That's the first impulse of anyone who has a heart. What we forget so often, though, is that it's important that we also take care of ourselves and honor our own passions as well.

A Harris Poll survey found that 80 percent of working Americans wake up every morning not happy, not fulfilled, and not passionate about what they do. I would guess that, more often than not, most of them have the disease of wanting-to-please-everybody-else-but-myself. So they give up their passion and their love in order to do what other people want them to do, or so that other people will love them. I've found that this doesn't work.

What keeps you going when things are tough?

I have three tools in what I call my "cosmic toolbox." I've been doing transcendental meditation ever since I was 20 years old, and that practice of gaining a deep state of rest, twice a day, keeps everything from *ever* being too much of a test. It doesn't mean that things don't get hairy, but when you're rested, life will always look a lot better. All this scientific research has found that by this regular practice of meditating twice a day, an individual gains a deeper state of rest than the state of rest gained in eight hours of deep sleep. So that's one of the first tools in my cosmic toolbox.

The second tool is that I believe every single moment is a gift—no exceptions. If I am looking at the world and it appears that it's against me or things are unfair, I use *The Work* of Byron Katie. She's got this wonderful process to take a look at limiting beliefs. What Byron Katie says is, "God is good, God is everything, and there are no mistakes in the Universe." If you're feeling pain, separation, or suffering, it's not the world that needs to change, but your thinking about the world that needs to change. Through Byron Katie's simple process of self-inquiry, I can turn those limiting beliefs around so I can see that everything is always a gift.

My third tool is The Passion Test, and I'm becoming quite an expert at choosing in favor of my passions. As you read, it was through trial and error. What I love so much is that when I choose in favor of the things that have the greatest meaning for me, not only do I win, but everyone around me wins as well.

What's been the most rewarding part of what you do?

The most rewarding part of what I do is growing more every day in walking my own talk, being the change I want to see in the world, and being the teacher who is living her teaching. I feel like, if each of us takes care of our own inner work, this is the greatest gift that we can give to mankind. If anyone is transformed through The Passion Test and the knowledge I share, that's a bonus. I really do feel that the most rewarding part is really standing for what I'm talking about and energetically being aligned with my own message. These aren't just vacuous words coming out; they come through every energetic particle in my body, and all of me is lined up with that. When I'm there, there's nothing more rewarding, because I know I'm giving all I can. I'm being all I can be. That feels so good, and it's so much fun to play in this beautiful creation.

What is the most inspiring transformation or manifestation that you've witnessed in your work?

All of us are constantly receiving gifts through the Creator, Higher Power, the Universe, whatever name you want to put to that energy that is greater than yourself. We're always being given new ideas and things. I was open enough to download The Passion Test, which is such a cool download because it is a system. The acronym for SYSTEM is *Save Yourself Time, Energy, and Money*. When I first started using The Passion Test to get myself out of my own Hell, I'd write passions like:

- When my life is ideal, I'm a world-renowned transformational leader.
- When my life is ideal, I am traveling the world first-class.
- When my life is ideal, I'm uplifting humanity.

And, as the years have gone on, I've used this tool every single day. The secret, as I mentioned, is that when you're faced with a choice, a decision, or an opportunity, you choose in favor of your passions. As I've done that, the most inspiring transformation or manifestation is the awareness that every time I choose in favor of things I care about, I'm saying yes to me. I'm saying yes to my own self-love.

I had a pretty tough life. I was physically abused. My mom, when I was little, was my best friend and then she became a massive alcoholic. I got hooked on drugs for a time in my teens, and I did some pretty radical things. I had friends who would say to me during those times, especially when I was taking drugs, "Janet, you need to love yourself more. You need to have more self-love!" And I thought: *Shut up!* I didn't know what that meant. If you're so far from yourself, people can scream it at you and try to explain, and it just doesn't compute. But as I started to get clear on what I was most passionate about, and I had the courage to choose in favor of those things, I realized that every time I said yes to me, I was growing in my own self-love.

The Passion Test is an incredible tool for each of us to really open up, flower, and bathe in our own loving-kindness, in our own love for ourselves. As we say, "This is what I stand for; I love you *and* I love me, and this is what I choose in favor of," then we grow in that love and become full. There's this beautiful saying in the Vedas: "From abundance comes abundance, and abundance remains." What's so beautiful is that as people grow naturally in their own self-love, they become so full, and in that fullness, they overflow. The natural, spontaneous progression of that overflowing is that one naturally has a desire to give. It's not based upon the mood of the mind; it's because we start becoming so aligned, as a tool in the hand of Nature, knowing that the secret to life is in giving.

The first baby step is the formula for living a passionate life:

- Intention
- Attention
- No Tension

Intention—use the Passion Test to get clear on what it is you choose to create in your life.

Attention—all of us are powerful; where are you putting your powerful attention? Are you choosing in favor of your passions, of the things you care most about? Are you saying, "I'm not beautiful enough, rich enough, smart enough, educated enough?" Are you turning on your TV and watching the news, filling your world with the negativity? What a samurai would do—and what I have learned to do as a conscious creator—is to consciously choose in favor of my passions and then take massive action. It's not enough just to say, "Om...I'm going to be a New York Times best-selling author." You have to do what you have to do. You have to sit down and write the damn book! You have to know what you're going to write about. Write the outline. What's the content?

Once you've done everything you know how to do, the last step of the formula is:

No Tension—surrender, let go, and say, "this or something better," knowing that in the "no tension" part, a vacuum state starts to be created where all people, places, and things start to show up to support you in living your passionate life. I don't know why that is; I just know that's what seems to happen in this beautiful dance called "the formula for living a passionate life."

Adam Markel

"I wake up every morning and I feel so blessed. I consciously, and unconsciously now, say to myself: I love my life!"

Adam Markel is the CEO for Peak Potentials and has been a trainer with the company for years. He is a Master Trainer in the areas of personal and business development, a keynote speaker, author, real estate developer, entrepreneur, and attorney. Having run his private law practice for more than 17 years, Adam focused his attention on creating a successful commercial real estate investment firm, title insurance company, and social media start-up. Returning to his roots as a teacher, Adam has now trained at Peak Potentials courses and camps for thousands of students in Singapore, Malaysia, Vietnam, Australia, Europe, Canada and the United States.

One of the most charismatic speakers you will ever see, Adam trains from his heart, believing that honesty and support bring out the best in people. He treasures the opportunity to be a role model to people who are looking to have amazing relationships, successful businesses, and time-freedom to pursue their life's missions. His strength of will, integrity, compassion, and natural leadership skills have helped to propel him into a successful role as a trainer, coach, mentor, and role model. He enjoys networking with other successful entrepreneurs and strives to reach out to those who are still struggling. Adam speaks his truth with compassion and finds strength in living authentically and passionately. One of his greatest joys has been raising four amazing children with his wife, Randi, and empowering them with these same traits.

To find out more: www.PeakPotentials.com

What personal event or universal problem made you want to do what you do?

I was in my mid-30s and my life was out of balance. I was working very hard, spending many hours each week in an occupation that didn't give me a lot of joy. I didn't feel as though I was living on purpose; I didn't feel connected to my heart in what I was doing. That lack of integrity, on my own part, caused me a great deal of personal pain. It was a springboard for me to look at how, not only to solve my own pain, but ultimately, to create solutions that worked for me and share those solutions with other people. That led me to what I am currently doing, as the CEO of one of the world's premier personal and professional development and success training companies, Peak Potentials, where I also train and help people to empower their lives.

What has been the hardest part of doing what you do?

The hardest part is, every day, just being true—being true to myself, authentic, and staying true to the things I teach. I need constant reminders just like everybody does. When I feel connected, when I feel in integrity, when I'm being authentic, when I'm connected to Spirit, when I'm connected to God…then my life works and feels good, and I feel *joy*. When I'm disconnected, detached, or just not feeling in touch with God, Spirit, and myself, then I'm in pain again. That pain doesn't go away permanently; it will rear its ugly head from time to time. The hardest thing for me is to really walk the walk and talk the talk. Doing the work is an ongoing process. That's sometimes challenging, but it's the only way I'd choose to spend my time because I know it truly works!

What keeps you going when things are tough?

Working on my spiritual side and wanting to be present with my faults, as well as the wonderful things I know I have inside of me to share with the world. What works for me is forgiveness. In the morning and in the evening, I spend a few minutes in a meditation that's divided into three parts—a simple formula, really. The first part is being in gratitude: being truly grateful for all of the blessings that I know are a part of my life and everyone else's lives as well. I have a lot of gratitude for being alive, for being here, for being present now—the whole mix. The second part of that process is forgiveness. I forgive myself for not being perfect or having all the answers, and I forgive other people for the same. The third part of that process is that I imagine myself being a mirror. I believe that God is love, so I radiate that love. I imagine myself as a lamp radiating that energy and love into the Universe, radiating love to my family, friends, and to people I've never met, to people all around the globe and throughout the Universe. I visualize a heart that is radiating this love energy, and other hearts radiating, vibrating, and lighting up around the world. I see that enveloping and wrapping the globe in this loving and warm energy and light. The process makes me feel good and brings me back to whole.

What's been the most rewarding part of what you do?

That's easy! I have been so blessed to be able to see people's lives change and transform. I realize that the word "transform" is quite a grandiose word in some respects, but it is absolutely true that as a trainer for Peak Potentials, and now being in a slightly different role with the company, I'm very committed to opening hearts. We're committed to our vision of the company positively impacting and transforming the lives of millions of people around the world. Having been able to see that actually occur—to see people's financial lives transform, to see people obtain their financial freedom, to see people whose health and relationships have transformed, people who are just happier, people who are living on purpose, who are mission-driven, all as the result of the work we do as a company and, to some extent, the work that I've done just by standing onstage and sharing with people my own life experiences—has been enormously rewarding and fulfilling. I wake up every morning and I feel so blessed. I consciously, and unconsciously now, say to myself:

I love my life! People will talk about creating the lives of their dreams, and I realize that my life has been, and is, better than my dreams were. That is pretty remarkable for me to be able to say, but it is definitely a statement about the service we're doing. It means so much that even the insecurities, issues, and petty personal stuff that we all have (and I have them, too), don't get in the way.

What is the most inspiring transformation or manifestation that you've witnessed in your work?

This will sound funny but…it's me! That's the one I know best. I went from working a grinding 70 to 80 hours a week, very much *not* loving my life and out of balance, on my way to some serious health issues. Then I watched as this work created a change in me. The way I've reinvented myself is no different from the way I teach others they can reach the same results. My story is: If I can do it, you can do it. I looked at people who had more balance, love, and purpose in their lives, and I modeled those people. I wanted to have more of what they had. Soon, I did some of the things that they were doing. I started to think and do things differently than I had previously. I took my ego, as best I could (and that's an everyday battle, as well), and said, "Okay, I don't know this. This isn't something that I necessarily know. I can do things differently, and if I do things differently, then maybe I'll have different results." Well, that's just what has happened.

I'm committed to my constant and never-ending self-improvement. It's been a blessing to see that in myself because now I recognize it in other people. It's hard to recognize things in anybody else if you don't first recognize them in yourself. For me, when I see somebody transforming, it reminds me of what I've been through, how far I've come, and how that process is still ongoing. You can see it in a person's eyes as they light up. We deliver our seminars all around the world, to hundreds of thousands of people, so, clearly, I get to see it firsthand…people who are, literally, sharing from their heart about things that have occurred for them…moments of realization when things have become clear, and when they've been able to do everything, including forgiving a parent, sibling, or friend for some grievance they had with that person from 20 or 30 years ago. People have held onto old angers and resentments, and they've been living with that poison in their bodies. I've been able to witness people relieve themselves of that poison and transcend some of the things that have been holding them back, in a major way, for a very, very long time. Then, of course, we've been able to witness people taking certain actions to create amazing results in their businesses, in their finances, and in their personal and professional lives, and that's been remarkable.

Dr. Joe Rubino

"What is so rewarding is that these people's lives are changed, just like flipping a light switch, when they map on these foundational principles and take them onto their lives."

Dr. Joe Rubino, CEO of www.CenterForPersonalReinvention.com, is acknowledged as one of the world's foremost experts on the topic of elevating self-esteem. He is a life-changing personal development and success coach on how to restore self-esteem, achieve business success, and maximize joy, fulfillment, and productivity in life. He is known for his groundbreaking work in personal and leadership development, building effective teams, enhancing listening and communication skills, life and business coaching, and optimal life planning.

His 12 best-selling books and audio programs are available in 23 languages and in 58 countries and include:

The Self-Esteem Book: The Ultimate Guide to Boost the Most Underrated Ingredient for Success and Happiness in Life

The Success Code, Books I & II

31 Ways to Champion Children to Develop High Self-Esteem

His highly acclaimed *Legends of Light* trilogy, consisting of, *The Magic Lantern: A Fable about Leadership, Excellence, and Personal Empowerment; The Legend of the Light-Bearers: A Fable about Personal Reinvention and Global Transformation;* and *The Seven Blessings: A Fable about the Secrets to Living Your Best Life,* are currently under development as feature films.

Dr. Joe's vision is to impact the lives of at least 20 million children and 20 million adults. His Certification Program training coaches in Self-Esteem Elevation is teaching people all over the world the tools to help children and adults develop high self-esteem without the problems associated with excessive ego.

To find out more: www.HighSelfEsteemKids.com & www.CenterForPersonalReinvention.com

What personal event or universal problem made you want to do what you do?

Actually, it was both a personal event *and* a universal problem. The personal event was that at 37 years old, I found myself experiencing this morose sense of, *is this all there is in life?* I had attended an introductory personal development lecture, and one of the speakers was asking, "What is it costing you to play small? What is it costing you to live your life in resignation?" At that time, my life was incredibly resigned and apathetic. Although I was very successful as a dentist—with my practice in the top one percent of all dental practices—I was unfulfilled. I did not enjoy what I was doing.

I wanted to answer the question about what it was costing me, so I decided to enter into a full-year personal development program, which ended up turning into a 10-year program. Over those 10 years, I discovered that the apathy and resignation I had been living in was costing me everything from my health, happiness, and life purpose (about which I hadn't been clear), to my ability to be fulfilled, share my gifts, contribute to other people, enjoy what I was doing, and be fulfilled in my work. So it was really costing me my life and my life force.

Now, over the course of the last 21 years, I've coached more than a thousand different individuals, and I've found that when they, too, were struggling and suffering and not enjoying life...whenever they were not abundant or not fulfilled, or their relationships were strained...whenever they were trying to numb out with drug or alcohol abuse...whenever they just weren't happy, or their communication was ineffective...all of these challenges always pointed back to the same underlying ingredient, and that was low self-esteem.

That pervasive, universal problem had me take on the challenge of creating a system to support people to elevate their self-esteem—a system in which they could connect the dots, and put into place whatever was needed to take their lives from wherever they were, to a much higher level, just by following some exercises, mapping them onto their lives, and seeing the transformation that I, personally, had discovered for myself 21 years ago.

So the process that I used to transform and enhance my life, I've now put into a simple, step-by-step program to allow people to transform their own lives. Low self-esteem is the universal problem, and I've taken it on as my life purpose to help people overcome it.

What has been the hardest part of doing what you do?

The hardest part has been the frustration of not being able to duplicate myself effectively enough to reach the number of people I want to reach. I've been holding onto the idea that if we can get enough people to elevate their self-esteem, and to raise their own consciousness, then we can absolutely raise the consciousness of the planet. When we help more people to be happier, and to relate better to others, there will be less violence, because there will be a whole lot less anger and sadness in the world. Then people can overcome worry and fear, get in touch with what really is important to them, manifest their own gifts into the world, live their life purposes, and access their dream lives.

I recently created two programs—one for children, and one for adults. These are certification programs in which I've taken the same principles that I've been able to teach adults and children, over the last 21 years, and now I'm duplicating myself by teaching other adults how to impact the lives of children and adults in these two programs.

It's been about six months since these programs have been introduced, and we've literally had thousands of people take on the challenge. We're creating legions of light-bearers, all around the planet, in every country of the world, who have taken on these principles and are using them to go into the schools, into the churches, on the soccer fields, in the boys and girls clubs, and with their own children and grandchildren.

So my largest frustration is now turning into my greatest satisfaction, with these same principles being used by so many, to duplicate what I was doing. And I'm absolutely clear that within the next 10 to 20 years, we're going to have a huge sequence of new generations coming in with elevated self-esteem, because of the work of all of these light-bearers.

What keeps you going when things are tough?

I keep reminding myself of why I'm here, and of the decision I made to step into the unknown, to risk, and to put myself out there (even though I was an extreme introvert) in support of other people making their lives work more optimally. The cost of not doing that keeps me going, when I realize that there are people who are "dead," like I was, and that if I stop my efforts, there's a greater likelihood that many of these people will not be able to gain access to some of the tools that I was fortunate enough to use and develop, to make my life work more optimally, and to impact others.

What's been the most rewarding part of what you do?

The most rewarding part has been impacting people's lives. I hear success stories about people whose lives were full of anger, and now they're full of love…full of worry and fear, and now they're stable and have positive expectations…people who were addicted to sadness, depressed people—

there are about 280 million of them around the world. When these people discover that they can manage their interpretations and overcome their depression, on a moment by moment basis, they can beat it. They don't need the drugs; they can get over them. They don't need the psychiatric care; they can get over that.

What is so rewarding is that these people's lives are changed, just like flipping a light switch, when they map on these foundational principles and take them onto their lives. They see that they can be in development, embrace problems, and look for the good in every opportunity. They can expect great things to happen and be self-motivated to achieve those great things, because they have that positive expectation for their future.

What is the most inspiring transformation or manifestation that you've witnessed in your work?

Well, there have been many. I'll give you two that really stand out from the rest.

One was a woman who had been in four abusive marriages. In doing some work with her, it came out that when she was eight years old, she had put on her pretty, yellow polka-dotted dress, and had gone next door, against the advice—and the rule—that her mother had established when she had specifically told her, "don't go next door."

This little girl was abused by the man who lived next door, her neighbor, and she decided, at the age of eight, that she was a bad girl, that people were mean and cruel, that they hurt you and abused you, and that she deserved the abuse, because she had disobeyed her mother when she had put on her pretty dress and gone next door.

Four marriages later—all of them to abusive men—the woman started to wonder why all the men in the world were abusive. Of course, she was only attracting abusive men, and she got to be right about what she had made up when she was a child: that she wasn't worthy of anything but abuse, that people were abusers, and that she deserved all the bad things that happened to her.

When this woman realized that she had made all of that up as a little child, and that a child can make a mistake and still be a magnificent little girl, she came to understand that she wasn't worthy of the abuse, the bad marriages, and all of the pain she had encountered. In fact, she was worthy of magnificence and happiness. She was worthy of enjoying a loving, nurturing relationship with someone who cared about her and treated her superbly.

The woman got out of the last of the four bad marriages and has since been in a rewarding marriage, to someone who treats her like a queen. She broke the pattern. She is now aware of her self-sabotage and how she was creating the abusive situations by—literally—provoking them, in order to be right about being bad and worthy of being treated poorly by people who treat you poorly.

That was one of the most phenomenal and very rewarding, transformations I have witnessed.

The other one was a person of color, who had grown up being picked on, bullied, and called all sorts of names and ethnic slurs. He became raging mad—indignantly angry—at being treated unfairly and poorly. He went through life with a huge chip on his shoulder. He was constantly in fights, constantly getting demoted or fired, and constantly in turmoil, everywhere in his life, because he got along with no one, and didn't feel like he belonged or fit in.

This man realized that he, too, had bought into some negativity about who he was. He had made up his mind that he was inferior—that he was not as good as other people. He realized that this was totally false and that he was worthy of happiness. He also realized that people were good at their core; they weren't how he had held them in his mind—as mean, cruel and disrespectful—but the majority of the people in the world were loving, caring, good people. He had the ability to manifest friendships and warm, loving relationships. He could treat people with respect and be treated, in turn, with respect.

The result was a total life transformation. Instead of working, day to day, to overcome the struggles of being in constant turmoil…instead of living a tumultuous life, always arguing and fighting, never getting along with anyone, finding fault with whatever people said or did, and looking to be validated all the time, this man gave up his right to be validated. He gave up his right to be inferior, and he's now at peace, for the first time in his life. Another incredibly rewarding transformation.

Lissa Coffey

"We are all connected and we are here to help each other grow."

Lissa Coffey is a lifestyle and relationship expert and a frequent contributor to "The Today Show" and other national television shows.

Lissa is the author of five books. Her new book is *Closure and the Law of Relationship: Endings as New Beginnings*. Deepak Chopra says: "Eastern philosophy teaches us that change is inevitable, and yet suffering is not. In her insightful new book, *Closure*, Lissa Coffey shows us how we learn and grow as we move through the evolution of our relationships. Highly recommended."

Lissa's best-selling book, *What's Your Dosha, Baby? Discover the Vedic Way for Compatibility in Life and Love*, does for Ayurveda what Linda Goodman's *Love Signs* has done for Astrology.

Lissa writes three different email newsletters and has more than 100,000 subscribers. She has several different websites, including www.CoffeyTalk. com and www.WhatsYourDosha.com. "CoffeyTalk: Ancient Wisdom, Modern Style" is an Internet television show seen on YouTube, iTunes and many online channels.

To find out more: www.CoffeyTalk.com

What personal event or universal problem made you want to do what you do?

The way I got started is kind of a roundabout story. In 1989, I was a young mom with two little boys who loved music. I used to play cassette tapes for them, and I thought: *If I hear "Old MacDonald" one more time, I'm going to scream.* There just weren't many options for kids' music. I thought: *This is really important, because kids at a young age, the first words they memorize are the words of a song. What are they learning if all they are memorizing is E-I-E-I-O? What does that mean?*

I looked all over for kids' music that I could stand to listen to over and over again, because you know how kids are. They don't want to just listen to a song once. They say, "Again! Again!"

I wanted good pop music that I liked, but with really positive messages for my kids, and I couldn't find anything. So, I thought: *Well, I'll just make it.* That's kind of the story of my life: *I'll just make it.*

I knew nothing about being a record label, but I did it anyway. I started writing songs and I found a collaborator who did the arrangements and the music. I hired some fabulous singers and we recorded these songs and came out with our record label, Bright Ideas Productions. It turned out great. Everybody loved it and all of a sudden I was in the kids' music business. I was doing shows at the mall, for the stroller set, and it was pretty exciting.

From there, I kind of became a parenting expert, and I got a job at a local TV station as their parenting reporter. They were a small, local station and they couldn't afford to pay me, so I asked if I could work in trade for them.

I said, "You give me production time and I'll do my parenting reports every week."

They were like, "Cool, that works out."

I used the production time to make music videos out of the songs. All of a sudden, I was in the production business, producing music videos. The music videos ended up running on Nickelodeon, the Learning Channel, and Discovery Kids, and they were really popular.

Then I wrote my first parenting book, *The Healthy Family Handbook,* and another one based on parenting and spirituality, *Getting There: Nine Ways to Help Your Kids Learn What Matters Most in Life.* I started getting calls to do national television shows, which was fabulous, of course! I did two shows, "Mike and Maddie" and "Carol and Marilyn," both of which aren't on anymore. It was before "The View" was on the air.

The work was fun, I really like doing it, and it kind of evolved from there. As my kids got older, my topics followed the path of my life. First, it was about personal growth, then we talked about relationships, and after that we talked about all these other things that women like me, and people in general, go through. It really evolved and I went with the flow. Once I got into the website stuff, it took off, because then we didn't just have a local audience, we had a worldwide audience. Then I started writing my newsletter and getting all these subscribers, and I'm like: *This is cool!* and I kept doing it.

What has been the hardest part of doing what you do?

The hardest part for me has been the inconsistency. There are times when I am so, so busy, I can't get enough done, and it's overwhelming. I'm just one person in this business. I don't have staff. I have two people who work with me on an as-needed basis; one is my video editor and one is my webmaster. So, other than that, it's just me. Then, there are other times I wonder when something is going to happen. I have to go out there and try to make things happen, and create.

What keeps you going when things are tough?

I think what keeps me going, more than anything else, is that I love what I do. I love the process of it. I love the creating. I love the marketing. I love connecting with the community. I love the research, exploration, and learning. I love every part about it. I even love the tech stuff, if you can believe it. When I find a new innovation, I see how I can use it to make the message louder, bigger, and have more reach. I just love every part of it. I can't think of anything else I would do if I weren't doing this. This is the perfect thing for me.

If you know about Ayurveda (because I talk about Ayurveda a lot) I am a Vāyu type. I am very creative. I like to do different things all the time. I'm not really a nine-to-fiver. This fits in with my lifestyle really well. I work at home, so I make my own hours, which tend to be really long hours but that's okay. I can multitask. I just love it, and that is what keeps me going.

What's been the most rewarding part of what you do?

The most rewarding part, for me, has been building the community and connecting with people whom I never would have met if I hadn't been doing this…people from all over the world who have really become a support system for me and the whole evolution of the company. They consider me a support system for them as well, and for what they are going through. I love that synergy. I love that we are helping each other. I love that we are the perfect example of the Law of Relationship, which is something I wrote a book about. We are all connected and we are here to help each other grow. That's what the community is for me, and that is what I hope I do for the community as well.

What is the most inspiring transformation or manifestation that you've witnessed in your work?

There are so many individual stories that people write to me via email. Sometimes I open up my email and read these stories and tears come to my eyes: *Wow…the power of the Internet…the power of this connection… thank goodness!* Whenever I get down, thinking that maybe my book isn't selling enough…well…it doesn't matter how much it is selling; it matters that the right people who need it are getting it. When I get letters from people, saying I really changed their perspective on things and they feel so much better about their situations and they've been inspired to make a change and do something new, I feel like: *Yes, that is what it is about!* That is really what fuels me so much and I love it.

I think a lot of the stories have centered around Ayurveda. I hope I'm one of the people at the forefront of making it a mainstream practice. I remember 20 to 30 years ago no one had heard of feng shui, but now everyone knows about it. It is part of our vernacular. Even if we don't practice it, we are a little bit familiar with it. Now I think that's how Ayurveda is. People are understanding it, using it, and applying it in their lives. I hope I've had some part in that as a Westerner, and as a woman who practices it in my day-to-day life. I hope to be an example of what this philosophy and lifestyle can do for you.

Joe Palmer

"More often than not, I'll shift simply by being of service to someone else."

Joe Palmer is a business and life coach, certified sales trainer, and teen leadership trainer with over 26 years of experience. His professional career began in 1986 at Jenny Craig International. Joe soon became apt in a variety of businesses such as insurance, property management, and international wholesale products, which included over a year at a Boeing subsidiary which specialized in manufacturing parts for U.S. fighter jets.

Joe's coaching career began in 2002 as a life coach with numerous personal development and leadership trainings. He found he had a passion and a natural proficiency for coaching and as his mastery was recognized, he was promptly recruited by SuccessTracs, a division of Peak Potentials, one of the world's fastest growing training companies headed by T. Harv Eker, author of *Secrets of the Millionaire Mind*. Joe subsequently was invited to complete a Business Coaching certification course with the company, being one of the select few chosen out of hundreds of candidates.

Working on the completion of his first book, *The Bullseye Theory*, Joe is currently growing his coaching and public speaking practice from the Northwest San Diego area. His poetry works and musical creations are published regularly. Joe's next book, *Help Wanted: Inquire Within* is currently under production and will be published soon.

To find out more: joe@bullseyetheory.com & (323) 309-6999

What personal event or universal problem made you want to do what you do?

About ten years ago (maybe a little longer), I went through a divorce, and at the same time I was in the height of my alcoholism. It was time for me to take a long, hard look at my life. It was time for me to be honest, real, and upfront about who I was, how I was in the world, and the results I was creating because of who I was being. That opened me up to focus on myself in a responsible way, and then it opened up a wide world of opportunity to be of service and help others.

The universal problem was that everyone else had the same kinds of problems I was going through…maybe not divorce or alcoholism, but struggles with their relationships, their businesses, being happy at work, their health, or whatever the case might be. It set me on a path to help others after I was able to help myself and take the learning, training, and coaching I received to get to that place.

What has been the hardest part of doing what you do?

There are a couple of hard parts. Firstly, maintaining responsibility. The good news is…now you know, and the not-so-good news is…now you know. It requires you to live up to, or be responsible for, your awareness. There are no more back doors or lies. There's no selling out, giving up, quitting, or playing small once you realize that's not how you want to live your life. There isn't another option. There are no more choices. Your commitment is: *I'm moving forward in spite of any barrier that will stop me.*

Another thing that's hard is finding the connection…meeting and connecting with people to whom I can offer these wonderful things that I've learned. I want to just give it away. The hard part is finding the audience to come and take the tools that were so freely given to me, that I so freely want to give back now. I want to stand there saying, "Here it is! Come and get it!"

What keeps you going when things are tough?

Firstly, it's music that keeps me going. I'll write music, I'll play, I'll sing, I'll listen to some old recording. It might not be music that I am associated with, but music that I appreciate.

Next, is the connection to my children—my son, my daughter, and now my granddaughter—and other family members. More often than not, I'll shift simply by being of service to someone else. I'll have a client call, or I'll be doing one of my teen trainings, or whatever the case might be, and no matter what's going on in my life, I can set that aside and be of service. The next thing you know, things resolve themselves because I stopped thinking about me and started thinking about someone else. That pulls me through all the tough times because I see that I'm "on purpose" now, instead of being "off purpose." Things are really tough for me when I'm not "on purpose."

What's been the most rewarding part of what you do?

The list is endless! With my clients, it's the successes they've had. Some have literally created millions of dollars or developed and grown their businesses to double and triple their income. Some have found how to master their own lives. I have one client whose big accomplishment, at least to start, was to have his wife's children connect to him. That was such a beautiful thing. He was a whole and complete person once he accomplished that, and he did not see *any* way possible when we started. When her children accepted and loved him and saw him as the father figure he wanted to be, I could have quit working right then and there, it was just so magnificent.

It's also rewarding to work with teenagers and see the transformations that occur in two days. Some kids come in the Saturday morning of our training with their hoods pulled over their heads. They're angry, they're bitter, and they don't want someone else to tell them what to do.

That's Saturday morning. Then Sunday night, their hoods are pulled back or not even on, their hair is combed, they're attentive, they're taking responsibility for their lives, they're swearing off gangs and drugs and committing to a career or going back to school. When I see that kind of transformation, I just feel so blessed. That's a reward and I can't be thankful enough for that opportunity. I say, "Thank you, God!" every time that happens.

What is the most inspiring transformation or manifestation that you've witnessed in your work?

I had a client who was a doctor. He was doing well in his career and wanted to take his business to the next level. He wanted to create a part-time business and bring in multi-millions of dollars for himself and his family, so he could put his kids through school. He wanted to get into real estate development and investment. It was a big game.

I had to ask him, "Are you sure you're capable and this isn't too big of a game for you to play?"

He answered, "I'm committed. I'm going to use all of the tools you've given me and we're *going to do this*."

In six months, he was signing his third contract for a business that he started from nothing, from which he received a million-dollar contract. Because of the contract he created, he was forced to buy property to house the people who were part of the contact. His real estate investments started taking off immediately, and his nearly-impossible dream came true.

Cheri Valentine

"The more people I can reach, and the more people I can help to find that spark within and to see themselves and their relationships, the more joy it brings me."

Relationships have been Cheri Valentine's life's work. From a very young age, she noticed how people interacted with each other and became fascinated by the dynamic of relationships. She has been exploring, studying, and living how to have relationships that are supportive, loving, and healthy for over 30 years.

It has not always been easy. Cheri has lived her own struggles and challenges with divorce, difficult personal relationships, and disabling illnesses. Yet, her choice to see these experience as gifts and use them for her own personal and spiritual growth has paved the way for her to help many others improve their personal, professional, and love lives. Using energy, intuition, compassionate listening, empathetic understanding, and insightful and pointed questions, Cheri mentors independent, strong, and successful women to connect to their divine self and learn to trust their inner wisdom and guidance.

Cheri has a BS in education, is trained as a Strategic Attraction and Relationship Coach, EFT Specialist, Passion Test Facilitator (also for Kids & Teens), and Energy Healer. She has a unique perspective into human nature and what drives people to, and holds them back from, love. Her real life experiences have led Cheri on her own path to love. She is now married to her soul mate and is passionate about helping you shine your unique love light so that you can enjoy lasting love and thriving relationships.

Cheri is the host of the radio show "Planting Seeds of Love" on www.A2Zen.fm.

To find out more: www.CheriValentine.com & (603) 967-4546 & love@cherivalentine.com

What personal event or universal problem made you want to do what you do?

This is a hard question to answer because there are so many components to it. As I go through my own growth and expansion, and continue to work with my clients, it becomes clearer to me than I even understood at the beginning. The universal problem, for me,—and it's very connected to personal events—is that my whole life, I felt a sense of responsibility. In particular, when my first child was born, I just knew, without a shadow of a doubt, that part of my purpose here was to change the dynamic of families and children and how that looked. So much of my inspiration comes from my brother and how I saw him suffer, throughout our life, growing up. He's been the light in my heart through my whole life, encouraging me to try to get things right and do things right. When my children came, again, it was time to do it for them, so they could witness, understand, see, and experience healthy, loving relationships…so they could see the light was inside themselves and believe, trust, and know that they could do anything they set their heart to do, and be filled with that sense of self-esteem. The driving force is my children and to rejoice in my brother.

I've come to understand that this purpose was always in me. I honestly think that if more adults would connect to that light within themselves and heal from the dysfunctional love they experienced and were taught, then they could change that and teach it to their children. I want it so badly for this world…for all of us to be connected within, from a place of love that's joyful, accepting and Sourced, rather than the way so many people have experienced love and come to believe that it is painful.

What has been the hardest part of doing what you do?

Initially, I think the hardest part was being able to separate myself from my clients and not take on the pain of others. I was very empathic and empathetic, and I didn't realize how much of my own health challenges— and my taking on other people's pain, worry, and hurt—affected me, not just in my everyday life but in working with my clients. That was very difficult because not having all the energy I needed all the time made it harder to do what I needed to do.

The second difficult piece was that I had Lyme disease; I was still healing and working through that very debilitating health challenge. One of the biggest areas impacted was my cognitive ability. I hadn't quite understood the capacity of that until I tried to create a bigger vision and get out there in a bigger way to help more people. That was really challenging and difficult as well.

What keeps you going when things are tough?

I connect to my heart, and I just ask why I'm here and why I'm doing this. I see this light of love and I know that I can't *not* do it. The more people I can reach, and the more people I can help to find that spark within and to see themselves and their relationships, the more joy it brings me.

What's been the most rewarding part of what you do?

There are two really rewarding things for me. The first is having watched my children (I still call them "children" and "my kids" because they'll always be my babies!) become these *amazing* adults, who are so well-adjusted and doing such amazing things. To see their growth, to see them step into their own spaces and have that sense of foundation that I finally feel I was able to help create, to see the relationships they have with each other, and to know that they see me in a different way, is extremely rewarding. To model something for them that I deeply believe in is *so* rewarding.

When it comes to my clients, the most rewarding thing is when a client says to me, "Cheri, I see now how I've been allowing this to happen. I've found it hard to pull away from something, and now I realize that I absolutely deserve to have a relationship and be loved and cherished the way that I want to be." When I hear somebody really make that shift within themselves, there's nothing better. That's the most rewarding thing ever.

What is the most inspiring transformation or manifestation that you've witnessed in your work?

I'm thinking of one woman in particular. When I think back to when we first met, my heart broke to see somebody who felt so broken and so alone...to see this woman having gone through a relationship that was better than anything she had ever experienced, and then having to deal with the ending of that, and being able to go in and see for herself the gift that it was—the ending of it and what that opened up within her; that was something she never could have seen or moved beyond. She started to look at all the relationships in her life and she saw how often she discounted herself, and how everything she did wasn't from the place of love she really wanted it to be from, but from a place of needing acceptance and hoping somebody would love her. When she saw that on her own, watching her blossom and make changes in her life has been amazing.

Glo Biccum

"The soul is our true source of information; it's the window to amazing insights and transformation when we allow ourselves to step into the darkness to find the light of who we really are."

Glo Biccum is a Certified Life Coach, a visionary, and a strong supporter for women achieving their dreams. Her over 30 years of nursing expertise as a healer has given way to being an advocate for woman seeking a new journey.

When Glo was in the process of leaving her corporate position in the medical field, many conversations happened within. She experienced self-sabotaging thinking, such as: *You can't do this, you don't have the skills, you aren't good enough, and you can't possibly be courageous enough.* She lived with "Super Woman Guilt" for years, juggling job expectations, personal time needs, parenting demands, and daily relationship requests, only to feel tired, overwhelmed and exhausted. Her self-denial had been creating pain and suffering, and it led her to shut down emotionally, spiritually, and physically, resulting in complete adrenal collapse. She was lost, but soon found herself on an amazing journey of introspection and healing. She made a decision to heal herself from within and when she stepped into the actions that supported that cause, her entire life began to heal.

Now, she shares the experiences and the tools she learned on her journey with women, from all over the world, who are searching for support and desiring to experience more happiness, joy, and pleasure in their lives. Using the tools and resources that Glo has created, you can transform your life. It's all about the willingness to take the journey, to heal from the inside, out. Are you ready to take this journey? Contact Glo to begin *your* journey today!

To find out more:
www.FireproofYourFeminine.com & fireproofyourfeminine@gmail.com

What personal event or universal problem made you want to do what you do?

There wasn't just one particular event or problem that led me to my venture in life; it was a culmination of *how* I was living my life that got me to where I am today. Overload, in the corporate world, consumed my life. I felt I never had enough time or money to achieve my desire for financial success and freedom, or my desire for the deeper wisdom of discovering who I am. I was trading time for money and never having enough time to make more money. For over a decade, I was being a very dedicated single mother of four wonderful children, continually having to rely on myself and my strong work ethic, and determined to provide abundantly for my family.

Then there was a crossroads and my life changed forever. I was rushed to the hospital in acute adrenal exhaustion. My body was depleted, emotionally and spiritually, and my endocrine system had no reserves to support, maintain, or nourish me. I had no more "fight or flight" in me, and I felt destitute and doomed to failure. This was a catastrophe in my life.

My nursing career came to a standstill, and since my identity had been all wrapped up in the medical work I did, I felt abandoned and alone. I needed support and I cried out to God.

At that point, an amazing man—a personal growth guru—showed up in my life. I worked with him weekly to explore the inner depths of who I was. Bob Proctor guided me through my transformation and, from then on, I have never stopped growing and learning.

I truly desired to have more women in my life who could understand and support me. If there is one thing for which I am deeply grateful, it is the insight that I needed to seek out a feminine perspective to help me access the pain and dissolve it. I attracted a mentor, from the feminine perspective, who shared many of the experiences that had broken me down, and who had also experienced a similar journey. Brenda Rivas, with her loving guidance, created realizations, breakthroughs, and an understanding of my power as a woman, not just as a wife and mother. I experienced a profound connection with my true divine feminine essence and discovered the hidden abilities of my heart.

Today, my work is about sharing and opening the door for other women who are feeling disconnected, confused, undefined, or undecided, and want to go to the next level of self-discovery. We carry the light to our own transformation when we embrace the power within ourselves, and it's the discovery of this power that becomes the transformational tipping point. The soul is our true source of information; it's the window to amazing insights and transformation when we allow ourselves to step into the darkness to find the light of who we really are.

What has been the hardest part of doing what you do?

The hardest part has been accepting what is. Life is not always easy and peaceful. I experienced lack, limitation, and struggle, and being okay with that was a very important awareness for me. I looked at these things as opportunities for transformational breakthroughs. Embracing the transformation brought me to the other side, and there was always a blessing on the other side.

I also learned that on the other side of fear, the fear always disappears. When challenges and opportunities showed up in my life, I was able to allow myself to feel whatever I felt. If I was scared, I could move to excitement. Instead of indulging my anxiety, I could awaken to my courage. There is nothing wrong with being afraid, as long as we do not let it stop us from doing the things that excite us. Most of us assume that brave people are fearless, but the truth is that we simply become more comfortable with fear as we face it on a regular basis. The more I could cultivate my ability to move forward instead of backing off, the more I could trust myself to be able to handle the new opportunity, whether it was a new job, an exciting move, or a relationship. When I felt my fear, I would remind myself that maybe I was actually just excited. I was able, moment by moment, to remind myself that every new opportunity has come my way because I was meant to experience it.

We aren't here to just get by and survive; we're here to step into our infinite abundance. That requires trust...trusting that it's all going to work out even *better* than I expected...just the way it's supposed to be! And it's really important to state what you want, because if we don't state what we want, then we are creating by default. So I state what I want, then release any anxiety and *allow* it to show up, and then I remain open to "this or better" showing up in my highest good. I might desire to have a new kitchen, and plan for all my appliances, widgets, and gadgets to be in a certain price point, but God and the Universe might have a plan to equip my kitchen with top-of-the-line goods. When I am being in the place of knowing what I want, and being in the place for that—or something better—to show up, then I get what I want.

What keeps you going when things are tough?

What keeps me going is that I really realize that I am *not* alone on this island...that there are so many people out there, on their islands, and they, too, are patiently waiting for a transformation. There are people who really care, who want to listen and want to actually hear me. They help me to step out of my emotional cave, the place that I have retreated to. It feels safer at first, but then it starts to get very lonely and dark in there. It takes a lot of courage and determination to stick my head out and have a look around, and it takes a stack more courage to step outside and stand tall amidst all of that uncertainty.

I've also learned that "a problem shared is a problem halved" every time… not just sometimes. The value of talking and sharing your stuff, with someone who actually does care and wants to help, is absolutely priceless. I have been able to access my wisdom through my experiences and have learned how to filter and download all of my new ways of being with the help of all those I have reached out to.

My biggest, and most valuable, team were my children. Their desire to see their mother succeed, and be free of worry and free of financial strain, was my absolute biggest motivator. They accepted me, believed in me, encouraged me, and celebrated me on my big wins (even when it was something small, it was still big to me). With their love, acceptance, and motivating words, I made it to the other side.

What's been the most rewarding part of what you do?

The most rewarding part of doing my work is witnessing the fulfillment of long-time dreams in women who were searching for their purpose, their passion, and their peace of mind…hearing that "aha" in their voices and experiencing that joyous moment with them, when they discover the reason they want to pop out of bed every morning, learn something new, and pay it forward to the next wonderful woman who comes into their lives. There is not one time when each woman I have coached has not been a teacher for me. There is always an exchange of wisdom between myself and the woman that I am mentoring; we each benefit from the session. I have been blessed to be able to create a deeper connection with like-minded women. We all experience challenges in our lives. It's not *if* we experience it; it's *when* we experience it. My journey was made possible by the loving financial contribution of my husband. I feel it is so important to appreciate the significance of risking everything to take the journey (and I know that you have people in your life who believe in you more than you believe in yourself). I was so blessed to have had my husband take that risk on me.

Another tremendous reward I receive from doing this work is the opportunity to create a legacy for my children, a generational transformation and evolutionary change to empower a future generation. Just like other women, I made mistakes with my children as they were growing up. I just did not know what I did not know. I am so grateful, now, that I can impart "new and improved" ways of being a better parent, managing a stressful situation with more clarity and certainty, and responding in ways that bring calm rather than calamity. As a single mom, I felt overwhelmed and seldom did I have someone I could turn to who could mentor me through my challenging moments. Discovering that there are other women out there—who face similar experiences and need loving support from a fellow goddess who understands their circumstances—has been extremely supportive and reassuring. My life experience is inspiring others to do greater, and to be greater, in their own lives.

What is the most inspiring transformation or manifestation that you've witnessed in your work?

The most inspiring are women who have learned to manage their fears and experience safety and trust with themselves, and women who have delighted in discovering their personal power.

I've transformed myself and my life by being of service to others. I realized that when I am authentic, I attract the people who are naturally compatible with me and it creates opportunities for them to truly get to know me. Allowing others to see who I truly am helped me develop the quality connections I always desired. And learning to give of myself, without expecting acknowledgment, helps me feel more empowered and inspired because I know that I've made a difference in someone's life.

When I release my expectations and adopt a more relaxed focus about my goals, it allows God and the Universe to orchestrate events in the best ways possible—even greater than I had imagined in the first place.

Letting go of my expectations invites God and the Universe to work on my behalf and create the circumstances that are best for me. The more I remember this, the more I simply enjoy the process of pursuing my goals without placing unrealistic demands on myself. I learned the hard way to step back and smell the roses. It took a physical breakdown of my body to discover that I was not responsible for the entire Universe, and that focusing on what I *can* control, rather than on what I cannot, allows me to let go of feelings like overwhelm and frustration. When I come from this place, I feel more empowered and I'm able to accomplish more than I would have if I had let stress dictate my actions. Now, I am able to take all I've learned and teach it to others in hopes that they will heal the pain they have within them.

I am confident that the words and stories I have shared here will inspire you to open the door to the next version of who you are becoming. You can move mountains if you believe in yourself and your dreams, and you take action. There will never be a better time than now. As you step up and say "yes" and invest your time, energy, and resources toward creating the life you were born to live, God and the Universe always respond with a big YES because you are taking a stand for yourself and your dreams. Are you ready to get started? Join the community of women who consciously choose to add *joy, passion, empowerment* and *freedom* to their lives! Let's get started today.

Cynthia Schwartzberg

"Watching the transformation, being a part of it, witnessing it, and knowing I've been able to support and help somebody are the greatest joys for me."

Cynthia Schwartzberg, LCSW believes that everyone has the innate capacity to heal, and that one's desire to heal is the cornerstone of any real change. She brings over 25 years of mental health experience as well as a lifetime of spiritually based seeking and learning.

Cynthia integrates various cutting-edge therapies into her practice called Cynthasis. One such process is Brainspotting, which she has been studying with its founder, Dr. David Grand, since its inception in 2003. In addition to being a Brainspotting consultant and therapist, Cynthia integrates mind/body therapies including EMDR (Eye Movement Desensitization Reprocessing), Core Energetics, and Hypnosis/Guided Imagery to support people on their journey to a more peaceful and fulfilled relationship to themselves, others, and life. She received her MSW from New York University and has completed various other post graduate trainings.

Cynthia is located in Atlanta, Georgia and is available by phone, Skype, or in person for individual and group sessions, teaching, and consulting.

To find out more: www.cynthasis.com

What personal event or universal problem made you want to do what you do?

The initial event that brought me into doing what I'm doing was my parents' divorce. I was exposed to therapy as a teenager and when I left that session with the woman, I thought: *Wow, I want to do that for young kids like me, and I really want to help people.* It was as if this light bulb went off inside me. Here was this stranger, outside of our family system, who was able to make sense out of this chaos. For this to have had such a strong impact on me as a teen, I must have felt really validated and seen by her, knowing that I mattered and I counted. The sad part was that because I was a good kid, I didn't get to go back often, but I knew that a seed was planted inside of me.

I remember going back to one of my friends and saying, "I really want to be a therapist."

Then, of course, they started telling me their problems, and I started developing my listening skills. As life went on, there were other things and other times when major milestones pushed me into therapy or pushed me into growing in one form or another.

The universal problem has to do with separation, connection, and valuing each other's existence, which is what this book is about. I think as a human being, I was going through that. I do believe that when healing happens, it happens in connection—connection to the self, to the other, to the environment, to Spirit…to something.

The other time in my life when there was a lot of separation was when I went off to college. I felt lost and depressed, and was introduced to the Pathwork. The material taught me a tremendous amount. It gave me a perspective of mankind, human relations, the light and dark of life, and the personality, and that led me back to wanting to be a therapist and starting to study mind-body work. It also gave me the greater perspective from which I work.

What has been the hardest part of doing what you do?

The hardest part has been really keeping myself in balance—keeping myself clear, grounded, and present. When I'm in session with somebody, I'm like the athlete who has to stay in the zone. The hard part is when I get thrown off because something happened in the relationship with the person, or there's something they're working on or dealing with that doesn't feel as cleared inside me. Therapy is the relationship between the two people, and I need to stay as grounded and present as possible, which has created a way of life for me whether I'm in session or not. Having a deeper understanding of the bigger picture, believing in the bigger picture, and having faith helps…in a sense, falling back into that and trusting that; some people might call it the connection to a Higher Power. Or, I go for my own help or healing with a therapist, a healer, or a guide—some kind of support.

What keeps you going when things are tough?

What keeps me going is really holding that bigger picture and having a bigger understanding that we're all connected, that everything's connected and related. There's always a lesson for me to learn and grow with. I get the support I need to do that because my mind can't figure everything out, and I can't will things into being. I trust that there's something larger than myself out there.

What's been the most rewarding part of what you do?

The most rewarding part is to know I make a difference. It shows up when I give a session to somebody who has problems with their stomach, and they connect to feeling their emptiness. Then they go home and write a children's book, and that children's book gets published by a primary publisher. So, I know that what happened in my office has a rippling effect.

I don't even know, half the time, what it is that I'm saying, but I'll say something like, "We need to keep it simple," and they'll help save women in Africa and help build safe places for other women in other communities, or they'll start a work project so that women can become self-sufficient in a foreign country. Because I said that one thing, they come back into my office and I know that they're there for support and strength so they can go back out into the world and do their work.

For me, to watch that rippling effect, or to watch somebody give birth and awaken to something they did not realize before, and get a new perspective to feel more whole and grounded—these tiny little moments of birthing and awakening—that's so rewarding! Watching the transformation, being a part of it, witnessing it, and knowing I've been able to support and help somebody are the greatest joys for me. It goes back to that feeling from my very first therapist, the importance and value of feeling connected and seen. When I can pass that on to somebody else, and then they can pass that on to the world, and hold the perspective that we're all interrelated and all interconnected, and we're all part of the world, the planet, growth, movement, and everything, it's just a thrill!

What is the most inspiring transformation or manifestation that you've witnessed in your work?

In my work, we work a lot with energy and consciousness. Everybody is connected and each one person is making a change.

One day in the office, one of my primary mentors and teachers, Dr. John Pierrakos, came in and tossed the *New York Times* across the desk, and said, "Look at all our hard work!"

It was the news about the wall that came down in Germany, and I thought: *Wow! That's true. That's something, if you look at it that way!*

It was a beautiful example of each one of us doing our personal work, and the cumulative effects of that. It's like the hundredth monkey theory; there are so many times—like when I'm sitting in session and it's kind of like I'm an athlete—when you're in that zone and it's almost magical, but you know that it's more than just magic. You're a witness to this unfolding experience!

Keith Leon

"No matter what I've been doing for work, for a business, or in my everyday life, it's always been about being of service to others."

Keith Leon is a multiple best-selling author, publisher, book mentor, and is well known as, "The Book Guy." With his wife, Maura, Keith co-authored the book, *The Seven Steps to Successful Relationships*, acclaimed by best-selling authors, John Gray and Terry Cole-Whittaker, and Keith authored the best-selling book, *Who Do You Think You Are? Discover the Purpose of Your Life*, with a foreword by *Chicken Soup for The Soul's* Jack Canfield.

Keith's writing has also been featured in Warren Henningsen's *If I Can You Can*, Jennifer McLean's *The Big Book of You*, Justin Sachs' *The Power of Persistence*, Ron Prasad's *Welcome To Your Life*, and many other books, including his latest bestseller, *The Bake Your Book Program, How to Finish Your Book Fast and Serve it Up HOT*, which he co-authored with Maribel Jimenez (co-creator of the Bake Your Book Group Mentor Program).

Keith has appeared on popular radio and television broadcasts, including "The Rolonda Watts Show" and "The John Kerwin Show," and his work has been covered by newspapers such as *LA Weekly*, *The Valley Reporter*, *The Minneapolis-St. Paul Star Tribune* and *The Maryland Herald-Mail*. Keith and Maura have been regular posters on *The Huffington Post* and have been featured in *Succeed Magazine*.

Keith's passion is teaching people how to go from first thought to bestseller! His passion is inspiring and teaching people to *finish* the book they've wanted to write for so long, and to help 1000 consultants, coaches, service professionals, and entrepreneurs do just that in 2012.

To find out more: www.BakeYourBook.com &
keith@bakeyourbook.com & (310) 594-3208

What personal event or universal problem made you want to do what you do?

Since I was young, I've always had a plan: I would be a rock-and-roll star in my twenties and thirties, an author and motivational speaker in my forties, and a film director in my fifties and beyond. So far, it's all come to pass. I didn't achieve rock star status to the masses, but I'm well known in the spiritual music world.

I'm in my forties now, so I've been writing, publishing, and speaking. By the time I reached forty, I had been a life coach for some time. One weekend, I was coaching at a Peak Potentials event called Life Directions. During the event, the coaches, who volunteer in support of the seminar attendees, get to stand on the stage, introduce themselves, and share what type of coach they are. This allows attendees to pick and choose the coaches who can most support them with life or business advice, or with processes or assignments, during the event.

Knowing that I'd be standing on the stage and sharing my 15 second pitch, I asked myself: *Who are the people I've had the most fun coaching in the last year?* I realized that I was really enjoying working with the clients who were writing books. At that time, I had already authored two books and during the second book, had learned about the business and marketing of books from all the greatest author mentors in the world. I had an epiphany because of my current inquiry and it was this: *Until I become as famous as the people who taught me the book business, it's my responsibility to support authors and teach the masses what I've learned.*

When it was time for me to share my 15 second pitch, I proclaimed, "My name is Keith Leon. I am a speaker and a multiple best-selling author. They call me "The Book Guy." They call me "The Book Guy" because

I will take you from first thought to bestseller." I had a line of people in front of me on every break for the rest of the event, and for hours after the event concluded. I was overwhelmed by the response. After the event, I did some research and discovered that eight out of every ten people want to write a book, but only .01 percent will actually do it. That is a huge market—eight out of every ten people—and reading this information motivated and inspired me to increase that number of actual authors through my personal efforts. In that moment, I chose to be a book mentor—to see aspiring authors all the way through their process, to keep them motivated while they were writing, and to teach them the business of books as they wrote. That's what I've been doing ever since.

What has been the hardest part of doing what you do?

My mentor programs do a great job of getting people writing and keeping them motivated during the process, and yet, sometimes the universe puts obstacles in the way of my writers. Some of them face the obstacles head on and, using the tools I taught them, they plow through the challenge and come out on the other side, still on course and writing! Once in a while, someone will let the obstacles take them out of the process altogether, and they quit the program. The hardest part, for me, is to stay unattached to each author's outcome. Letting them go has proven to be tough for me on some occasions. I get to know my students. I know what they are writing about and what group of people will be inspired or motivated by their book, and when they give up before completing something so powerful, it's sometimes a challenge for me to let it go.

What keeps you going when things are tough?

What keeps me going is my inner knowing that I'm on course. I know, without a shadow of a doubt, that I am doing exactly what I'm here to do at this time in my life. Do I sometimes forget for a few minutes? Sure I do. But I'm blessed to have learned to notice the red flags that fly, all over the place, when I'm straying from my mission or coming from a negative space. When I find myself feeling down or being pulled in a negative direction by someone around me, I stop, close my eyes, take a breath, and ask myself: *What is the truth in this situation? How can I be more loving in this moment?* This pulls me back into the truth.

Prayer and meditation have been incredibly useful for me when things are tough. The times when I have thoughts of lack, negativity, or fear are the times my faith needs to be the strongest. Prayer and meditation are, for me, a powerful way to remember the truth and to remind me to be faith-filled, because I truly know that if I just hang on, no matter what is going on, it will pass. I know, from personal experience, that the worse things appear on the outside, the closer I am to a major breakthrough.

What's been the most rewarding part of what you do?

When I see pictures of my students holding their completed books, or when they send me signed copies of their books, that is very rewarding. I have worked with some authors from the point where they just had an idea for their books, through the whole writing process, all the way to them creating best-seller status for their books, using the tools and strategies I teach. One woman bought my home study course, implemented what she learned listening to my previously recorded classes and using the provided templates, and she had an Amazon Best Seller the day her book launched.

In my Bake Your Book Group Mentor Program, I do question-and-answer calls with the writers every other week, and sometimes the students are brave enough to talk about their challenges, obstacles, or their mind chatter (in our program we call that voice "the little liar"). I have an extensive background as a relationship expert and self-growth facilitator, so I work with authors on their challenges right there on the call. There is nothing more rewarding then hearing someone have a major shift on one of those calls. You can hear when it happens. All of a sudden, they inhale deeply and you can literally hear the "aha" moment happen! That is a very rewarding part of what I do.

What is the most inspiring transformation or manifestation that you've witnessed in your work?

My life is so amazing. In my work, I get to see transformation and manifestation happen all the time. One does come to mind for me and I'll share it with you. On one of the question-and-answer calls in my group mentor program, there was a particular student who had always participated at her 100 percent on the live calls. She would compliment the program, and my work, on every call.

We were about two months into the program when she said, "May I come clean about something with you, Keith?"

"Of course, you can," I replied.

"Keith, I love these calls. I come on the calls and get all fired up, then you do the process to send us off to write, I hang up, and when I put the pen to the paper, nothing comes out. I, literally, have written nothing since the course started. I understand the process, you motivate me, you inspire me, and yet…I've got nothing!"

I asked this student if she'd like to get to the bottom of it, right then and there. She agreed, so I proceeded to ask her a series of questions. During my inquiry, she started to get in touch with what was in her way. With each new discovery, I would dig deeper to see what was underneath it.

At one point, I heard my student breathe in deeply; it was that "aha" moment I spoke of earlier. She discovered what had been in her way all along. She cried tears of happiness because I had helped her reveal a very old paradigm based on something she had long since buried and forgotten. She apologized to the group for "taking so much time."

I opened up the line to ask if anyone felt she had wasted their time, to which the group members replied, "No way! Thanks so much. I learned so much. That's been getting in my way, too. I'm crying over here. That was so deep and so beautiful."

People continued to give her props for being brave and helping them see that we all have the same "stuff" that seems to take us out, and I reminded them all that we're more alike than we are different. When we strip away all of the layers we cover ourselves with for protection, and reveal the core and essence of who we truly are, we all want the same thing—to love and be loved. No more, no less…to love and be loved. Everyone learned something that day, and it was beautiful. This is why I do what I do…for moments like that.

I'll have you know that the woman who was willing to step up, face her fears, and burst through her "story" that day wrote her whole entire book in the two weeks that followed. She blocked out her calendar, told everyone not to call her, used the tools I taught her about how to marathon write, and wrote her book in two weeks. That is a true testament to how quickly a book can be done when you have a clear "why" and the drive to make it happen quickly.

Every three months we complete one of our courses and the last call is called a "celebration call." This is when all of the writers come with a list of their victories (no matter how big or small they think they are) and we celebrate. I love this call, because I get to hear how much progress people have made and support them with suggestions for next steps. On the celebration call, people, whom we may not have heard from since the beginning of the course, will share that they had been listening to each of the calls after the fact (from the recordings) and have implemented what they learned. It's amazing to hear how much writers can accomplish with focus, dedication, and a mentor teaching them. I love my work.

No matter what I've been *doing* for work, for a business, or in my everyday life, it's always been about *being* of service to others. My passion is *being* of service to humanity, and my life has clearly been about allowing Spirit to show me all the ways I can serve. How may I serve you?

Marcia Wieder

*"To manifest big dreams, you must be willing to take risks.
To take risks, you must trust yourself."*

Marcia Wieder, CEO and Founder of Dream University®, is leading a Dream Movement. With over twenty years of coaching, training, and speaking experience, her inspiring message has touched audiences of 50 to 5,000 at companies such as AT&T, Gap, and American Express.

Appearing several times on "Oprah" and "The Today Show," and in her own PBS-TV special, Marcia has been able to share her message with millions of viewers. She is a best-selling author and has written 14 books dedicated to helping people achieve their dreams. She also shared her passion for dreaming as a columnist for the *San Francisco Chronicle*, where she urged readers to take "The Great Dream Challenge."

Marcia believes there are the dreams we have for life, and there are the dreams life has for us. Everything we live through, our greatest successes and most painful losses, mold us to be uniquely us, encouraging us to live on purpose and in integrity with our souls. So, the question becomes, "What's important to you, and what are you willing to do about it?"

This year, she is committed to helping one million dreams come true. Although many would say this is a time to be realistic, she believes it's never been a more important time to dream. Connected to our dreams, we are empowered and in control of our destiny. A world that dreams has hope and, in that state, miracles occur. Marcia encourages you to believe in your dreams not because there are guarantees, promises, or assurances, but rather because they matter to you.

To find out more:
www.MarciaWieder.com & www.DreamUniversity.com

What personal event or universal problem made you want to do what you do?

There are four events. One personal event happened very early in my life, and then three more recently.

The year I was born, my older sister, who was five years old at the time, lost her hearing and became deaf. The story around the house was, "She must be jealous of the new baby, so she's not listening."

As my sister grew older, she became progressively more handicapped. My family lost its faith and its hold, and there was a lot of sadness around the home. Unconsciously, I became "Suzie Hope," the bright light within my family. I would say things like, "You can do it! Don't be stopped by obstacles. Go for your dreams! You can be happy!"

Then there was a moment, later in my life. I had written 14 books, I'd been teaching for almost three decades, and was considered a thought-leader on dreaming big and visionary thinking. The stages were getting bigger and bigger, and I had appeared on Oprah's show multiple times. But on a certain level, my work was becoming less and less meaningful. It wasn't until I started an inner journey, looking at what was driving me, that I realized that the person whom I wanted most to see and hear me wouldn't see or hear me on a stage or on Oprah—it was my sister. Not only was she deaf, but as she got older, she developed blindness. It was at that point in my life when, instead of being motivated by my wounds or loss, something really did turn inside me and I became much more mission-driven. I became personally more fulfilled by what I was doing, which then allowed me to have an even greater impact on the world. As a result of that experience, one of the basic principles I teach is: *Can you believe in something, not because there are promises, guarantees, or assurances, but because something really matters to you, and are you willing to take action on it?*

More recently, I bought a house in Northern California (overpriced, but with a million-dollar view!) The previous owners failed to disclose that the house had slipped eight inches on the foundation. Instead, they built a false floor to cover it. It was a nightmare for about four years—it sucked all my money out and there were lawsuits—until one day I finally said, "No more! I'm not living this way anymore!"

I wound up selling it as a "tear-down," which was a complete blessing. However, before I sold it, I bought another house, even though I couldn't afford it and everyone—mortgage brokers, realtors, parents, and colleagues—told me not to.

"You have to sell the old house as a tear-down before you can buy a new house," they said.

So, I started affectionately referring to it as the "Myth of Prerequisite:" A doesn't necessarily need to come before B. I had taught people not to look in their checkbooks for evidence that their dream was a good idea. Could they demonstrate they were really serious about the dream by taking action even when it didn't look like the right time or the smartest thing to do? I was receiving a big dose of my own medicine.

I realized that you have to be willing to step into the abyss for the Universe to get that you're really serious about your dream. Nothing in my life changed me more than this single realization. If I didn't go for my dream, if I didn't practice what I preached, even though it didn't look like it was a good idea, it was pretty much over for me. I would have been a hypocrite; I wouldn't have been able to teach, speak, or write about what I taught if I wasn't willing to live it in the face of a million-dollar threat. I did go for it, and it changed who I am, how I teach, and my ability to take greater risks. To manifest big dreams, you must be willing to take risks. To take risks, you must trust yourself. The thing that either erodes or deepens my own self-trust is how I make, and keep, my agreements—not just with others, but with myself.

The final piece, about humanity, was that I kept seeing people who were unhappy. I see a lot of people who complain, whine, and moan, and I've been one of them so I can relate! I think that the message of dreaming, of actually going for your dreams and redefining what it means to dream, has never been more relevant. The message of this work is: *Don't wait for evidence. Don't wait until you retire, the kids leave, or you have extra money.* It's all about going for your dreams because they matter to you.

I look around and I see a lot of victim mentality, sadness, and loss, and I know there is a reality where that's going on. I'm not Pollyanna or pie-in-the-sky, but I think that with our dreams—not just *having* them but *acting* on them—we take personal responsibility for ourselves and start to feel empowered again. We can restore dignity and faith, and maybe even transform the American Dream back to its original luster, not just for immigrants coming from outside the country, but for those who live here and want to create lives that really are in integrity with our hearts and souls.

What has been the hardest part of doing what you do?

The hardest part has been the cynicism. As a nation, we've stopped dreaming. We've become overly realistic. We're so mired in living from our clocks and calendars and bounced bank accounts that we don't even know what our dreams are, much less how to accomplish them! The baby boomers get more interested when I show them medical studies demonstrating that people with passionate dreams live seven to ten years longer. There's so much propaganda that misuses the word 'dream,' that it has become watered down: *We're the custodians of our customers' dreams; We're here to finance your dreams; The Ultimate Dream Machine.* It's challenging to convince people—sometimes being the lone voice—

that not only is it important, but there's never been a better time to go for our dreams. To inspire people to believe in themselves, and to have the courage and resources to act on those dreams, has been challenging.

We put up a website called *The Million Dreams Campaign*, and it's completely free with community support, tools, and resources. We're getting the traffic, but I was curious why people weren't registering their dreams.

I was with Jay Abraham, from Guerilla Marketing, recently, and he said to me, "It's a really big ask."

I wondered, "Why? We're not charging them anything."

And he said, "You're asking them to share their hearts, their secrets, something even they're not sure they believe in."

So it's a challenge to encourage people to take the first courageous step, especially during a challenging economy. Really inspiring people to get comfortable with uncertainty is such a critical skill to develop during these crazy, challenging, unusual times.

What keeps you going when things are tough?

What keeps me going is that I feel very mission-driven. I have a spiritual practice in the morning; I check in with God—or however that occurs for those reading this: Source, Spirit, Jesus—I check in and try to keep my ego in service to my soul, rather than my soul enslaved by my ego. I have good people around me who don't let me take my own "P.R." too seriously. I place a very high value on joy, and I use that as my barometer. Last year, I was pushed to grow a very big company, and noticed I was stressed all the time. I was eating, drinking, and sleeping: work, work, work! What I know about myself is that I really have a value on quality of life, so I want to build a lifestyle business.

One of my missions is to teach about dreams, but I'm not about the future. I'm not about: *Where do I want to be in ten years?* or *How much do I want to sell my company for?* I'm much more about: *What do I want to do today, and what's going to make me happy today? How can I contribute or be in service?* I'm on the board for Make-a-Wish, and that really sustains me. Now that I've moved to Beverly Hills, I can walk over to their office, which I really love.

I think what keeps me going is knowing I'm living in integrity with my soul and making a contribution to another person's life. I did a fundraiser recently, for Make-a-Wish, in which I raised $80,000. I *loved* asking for money for somebody else!

What keeps me going is just being happy, spending quality time with family and friends, having meaningful conversations, and some level of feedback that shows me that my life is making a difference, even if it's in some small way. Not all dreams need to be Mother Teresa "save the world" dreams. Your dream of quality time with your friends and family, your dream of being paid well for doing what you love, your dream of being healthy and physically fit, your dream of coaching or mentoring the next generation of dreamers…for me, those are the kinds of things that are really meaningful. In one word, *meaning* keeps me going.

What's been the most rewarding part of what you do?

The most rewarding part is getting thank you cards and Christmas cards from strangers who say, "I heard you," "I read your book," "I did your online course and it helped me," "It made me happier," "I lost weight, "I made a career change," "I'm a better parent to my children." Small things like that are fulfilling. It really is about making a difference. I love being a good girlfriend, a good aunt, or a good sister. I like being tired when I put my head down on the pillow—not exhausted, but feeling like that was a day well-used. That's really satisfying.

On a personal level, I've lived in a lot of different places: I lived in Cairo, Egypt when I was 25; I've lived in New York and San Francisco, and now Beverly Hills. It's rewarding to feel that I get to guide and direct the course of my life. That's really it. Even if it's something as simple as deciding I want scrambled eggs versus over easy, or I want to go take the dogs for a walk or for a run, there's some sense of perfection that I get to have a say in how my life runs and is created.

What is the most inspiring transformation or manifestation that you've witnessed in your work?

Living through the nightmare with my house was the biggest personal transformation, because I got to experience the difference between belief and faith. It's a whole other level.

I worked with one woman who went from a size 14 to a size 6, and five years later, she kept the weight off. It wasn't so much the weight loss as it was the mindset shift. With her newfound body, she started valuing and appreciating herself, and that gave her greater clarity and courage. She started her own business in her 50s, then she fell in love and got married. She said the whole thing started by coming to one of my workshops and believing in herself. So, from the 70-year-old woman I helped become a professional photographer after 25 years of being an amateur, to the woman who had passion for Italian food and moved to Italy to start a walking tour and picnic company in Tuscany, the key factor is that they believed in themselves.

A lot of people call me the "Enrollment Queen." Different from selling, enrollment is when you share your vision, product, or service in a way that inspires other people to join you, maybe even invest in you. The obstacle called "not enough money" disappears when people are enrolled by you and your vision, because they can contribute and invest in you. I think the number one thing I'm here to "enroll" people in is believing in themselves. I teach: *Can you believe in something because it matters to you?* That's a muscle to develop. That's a practice, because most of us want guarantees, promises, and assurances. I've watched, and coached, people with *no* money go further in life, sometimes, with their passion and commitment, than people who have skill and gobs of money. The stories go on and on.

One of the most inspiring stories, recently, was Claire, a 14-year-old girl with cystic fibrosis who, hooked up to an oxygen tank, was the opening speaker for the Make-a-Wish Foundation.

She said, "God gave me a short time to remind you guys to wake up, hurry up, and go for your dreams."

She was filled with joy about it; she knew who she was and why she was here. She wasn't transformed by me—I was transformed by her. My job was easy to speak after her, for half an hour, and then ask for money. I raised $80,000 for the Make-a-Wish Foundation in a couple of hours!

The most inspiring stories are the everyday people, like you and me, who, regardless of what's going on in the economy, instead of watching their retirements dwindle away to nothing, are still writing books and pursuing a dream of doing a television show. Even though people say to us, "Are you crazy?" we don't care. We're joyous in just pursuing the dreams of our hearts. I get to make a difference by being a role model of what it means to go for your dreams…by moving to different cities, trying different things, course-correcting, changing my mind, saying "no more" and "no, thank you" to what's no longer true, so I can say "now what?" to what I really want…to how I really want my life to be.

Health & Wellness

Dr. Sammy Pyon

"I have faith in the intelligent design of the Universe that we are co-creators of our reality and that the Universe is out for our highest good."

Dr. Sammy Pyon is a Chiropractor and a wellness doctor focusing on helping people obtain optimal health and wellness. He takes a holistic approach to healing and says, "We believe that wellness is experienced when the mind, body, and spirit are in harmony. When this is achieved, we enter into a state of abundant vitality, strength, joy, and peace. We seek to assist people in bringing harmony back into their lives so that they may align to their true purpose."

Sammy graduated from UCLA in 1990 with a Bachelor of Science in Kinesiology and from the Los Angles College of Chiropractic in 1995. He practices alongside his wife, Audrey, who is a Spiritual Relationship Coach, at El Segundo Family Chiropractic. Together, they offer an Evolutionary Experience in Healing in mind, body, and spirit. Sammy is a student and mentor of spirituality, philosophy, shamanism, new science, and the evolution of human consciousness.

"When my wife, Audrey, and I decided to open our office in 2003, we wanted people to have an experience unlike any they'd ever had in a doctor's office. Now, I think our aspirations are even higher; we want people to have an experience unlike they've ever had, period. We want people to find themselves in a caring, loving atmosphere because we honestly believe healing begins the second you walk in our door and continues on long after you walk out."

To find out more:
www.ElSegundoFamilyChiropractic.com & (310) 322-1757

What personal event or universal problem made you want to do what you do?

I don't think it was an event or a universal problem that I perceived at the time. When I was very young, I remember my mother wanting me to be in the healing field.

At the time, because I was so young, I interpreted it as her wanting me to be a doctor, but later in my life we spoke about what I was doing and she actually told me, "That's exactly what I wanted you to be. You thought I was just telling you to be a doctor, but I really wanted you to help other people heal in their lives."

So I've always had that underlying current with me—and I always felt something else pulling me, too. Throughout my life, I've always been pulled toward spirituality, metaphysics, quantum mechanics, and philosophy. I had a couple of spiritual epiphanies; one was at 19 and another around 21. There were several after that, but those two were the huge ones that really connected me, spiritually. The first one, I could barely make heads or tails of. It was such an incredible experience that I processed it for years afterward. The second experience led me to discover my first mentor, Terence McKenna. A large part of my life has been invested in processing this incredible spiritual energy that was released at the time.

I got into my profession in a surprisingly mundane way. I was a kinesiology major, at UCLA, with an exercise physiology emphasis. I enjoyed sports and ended up getting into personal training and rehab, so, I was working at a chiropractic office doing just that.

The chiropractor in the office asked me, "Why don't you become a chiropractor?"

I look back now, and I don't think I gave choosing a career as much thought as I should have. I just thought: *Sure, why not? It's right in line with the sports field I enjoy and maybe I can become some sort of sports chiropractor.* I really had no idea what the chiropractic profession was, at the time. I literally didn't know one thing! I had gotten adjusted but the chiropractor I knew was mainly a neck and back pain doctor, so, I really didn't get what a chiropractic adjustment was—what it actually did—until I started to learn about it in school and that was only on a mechanical and scientific level. But, as I was going through school, I began to hear all these great teachers, mentors, and chiropractors who had come before me talking about the true philosophy of chiropractic. At first, I didn't tie that into my own spiritual experiences. In fact, I was a very mechanically-oriented chiropractor, even beyond graduation, because I didn't tie spirituality into chiropractic. I see, now, that it completely and utterly goes together, and has intertwined so intricately in my life, because I believe chiropractic *is* a spiritually-based profession. We believe that the power that *made* the body *heals* the body; that very Life Force—that Innate Intelligence— courses through our spine, out through all our nerves, and into every single cell in our bodies. Chiropractic and my epiphanies came together, pulled me—in a spiritual sense, guided me this way, and then it was the perfect situation to be in when I found myself. When I woke up from the social programming of how we are supposed to fit into society and discovered more of my authentic self, I realized I had found myself in a profession that was perfectly suited to what I was meant to be doing. There was a lot of guiding, I believe—that I didn't even know about at the time—that was pulling me to where I am now.

What has been the hardest part of doing what you do?

The hardest part is maintaining the balance of not taking responsibility for a person's healing—ultimately, recognizing that they're the healer. I am merely here to be a facilitator. But, that's been difficult because I'm always striving to become a better chiropractor. There's always the component of *I can be better* and yet, at the same time, I have to let go of the idea that I'm the one healing them. I can be a better facilitator but, ultimately, they're the ones who heal.

On the opposite side of that has been taking too much responsibility for my perceived lack of healing in someone for whom I felt that, maybe, the outcome should have been different...maintaining that balance and continually working on myself to remember that I will always do my best, but without taking responsibility for a person's healing or for any perceived non-healing that goes on in my own mind.

What keeps you going when things are tough?

The main thing, I would have to say, is my family. My wife is the main person in that. She's an amazing, amazing coach. Part of the difficulty is that we see a lot of patients with different types of things going on in their lives; it's not just neck and back pain. We've lost people with cancer, and other serious illnesses, and those are the times when I completely break down and feel like: *How can I go on when I couldn't do enough?* Audrey's always been there for me and, every single time, has seen the good in me. I owe my life to her. If she had not seen the good in me, there's no way I would be the person I am today. Her support, as well as that of my friends and family, has been incredible.

I've also discovered amazing mentors and coaches in chiropractic. Dr. Steve Hoffman, who's an incredible chiropractor and an inspirational coach, has been a great influence in my life in both chiropractic and philosophy, and in my life and growth as well. So, by turning to my mentors, turning to support, and the vision I was given from my spiritual epiphanies, a vision of a higher dimensional shift in consciousness, I'm here to midwife that vision for the highest good of all beings, the Earth, and the Universe. I have faith in the intelligent design of the Universe that we are co-creators of our reality and that the Universe *is* out for our highest good. Terence McKenna once said, "I believe the best story will win out in the end." Holding a vision of the highest outcome for *all* concerned is the best story, in my opinion. Because we are co-creators, we should create the best scenario for the future of humanity, not the gloom and doom scenario. Faith in this vision has kept me going through the tough times.

What's been the most rewarding part of what you do?

There are so many victories and rewarding moments, throughout the day, when I feel like my wife and I have touched people in a truly positive, connected-to-Source way. That has been a daily reward. The fact that we get to share and celebrate each other's wins, at the end of the day, is a complete and utter blessing.

The single most rewarding event was when my daughter was born, just over three years ago. She beat incredible odds to be born. When she was born, I was in the delivery room and she was carried over to me to cut the umbilical cord. As she was being carried toward me, she opened her eyes and saw me for the first time with her blue eyes (her eyes were blue, at the time, and they're brown now). I cut her umbilical cord and as I carried her to my wife, Audrey, I gave her her first chiropractic adjustment and reconnected her to Source, the moment she was born, where she has been ever since. For me to have gone to school, studied, received my degree, and become an even better chiropractor over the years—just to be in that moment where she was born and be able to reconnect her to her Source—that was a phenomenal moment for me! That the Universe conspired to make this so for my daughter is nearly unfathomable.

What is the most inspiring transformation or manifestation that you've witnessed in your work?

I have to say that there have been a lot of issues and problems we've helped people overcome—and, believe me, I have so much gratitude for being a conduit and facilitator for that—but one of the biggest transformations we're seeing now is that people are recognizing the combined work that my wife, Audrey, and I do. She's a spiritual relationship coach. People are recognizing that our work, when combined, is not only about resolving symptoms or problems that people don't want any more but, rather, choosing something that they do want—the future they want, one of health, happiness, and joy—something they've always wanted, rather than just going along with life. Our work seems even bigger to me, because I have so much enjoyment in helping people with their issues, but now I see we're both helping people truly create the lives and health they want.

When I first started out as a chiropractor, I remember telling someone my intention was to get rid of their pain. That was the highest intention I held because I didn't know any better. Through the years, my intentions have changed completely so that now my intention, as I'm adjusting people, is to reconnect them to their Source and to the Innate within so they can be healed from within. That intention has changed completely and I think that corresponds to the changes we're seeing—the manifestation and transformation—in the world with consciousness rising. I do believe we're headed toward a higher-dimensional shift in consciousness. In the past year, we have seen more and more light workers, in our practice, seeking chiropractic work. I know that it's a direct reflection of our own transformation. We need to support light workers because we're all here to hold a vision of unity. So, I'm holding that vision as part of my spiritual and chiropractic work.

Dr. Steve Hoffman

"I believe I'm put here to inspire. Not just to help people get rid of problems that they have and don't want but rather to help people create the lives that they want but don't yet have."

Dr. Steve Hoffman is a visionary, a renegade, and a wellness marketing expert with a résumé that includes, but isn't limited to, 35 years in chiropractic—one of the largest wellness-driven chiropractic practices in the world, past President and Chairman of the Board of the Michigan Chiropractic Council, recipient of the One Concept Lifetime Achievement Award, and founder and developer of HealthPlus, a multi-disciplinary wellness-driven practice in San Diego, California. Dr. Hoffman offers a level of expertise in wellness-driven chiropractic technique, technology, practice building, and management. If there's one man, on planet earth, capable of ultra-simplifying the truth about success in the wellness-driven chiropractic practice, so both the doctor *and* patients "get it" instantly, it's Dr. Steve Hoffman.

As President of Discover Wellness, Inc., Dr. Hoffman's purpose is to help practitioners create the lives, businesses, and practices that they want. Success in life, business, practice, finances, relationships, and more all have common denominators. Success in any of these areas is a process which requires that all the necessary elements be present within the right hierarchy. If any of these key elements are missing, then success becomes elusive. Dr. Hoffman guides you through the process with practical products, technology, and coaching services.

Most recently, Dr. Steve Hoffman teamed up with Dr. Alan Weinstein to create a media and marketing company serving all businesses wishing to get their message into the hands of their public. The technology they have created bypasses the now passé issues associated with email and delivers your message directly to your audience's computer desktop screen.

To find out more: www.DrSteveHoffman.com & www.MC2Technic.com & www.YourContentBank.com & drsteve@drstevehoffman.com & (760) 208-1895

What personal event or universal problem made you want to do what you do?

It was a series of events. Everyone was dying and it wasn't a good thing. My mother's mother died in her forties, my mother's father died in his sixties, my mother's brother died in his fifties, and my father's brothers all died before the age of sixty. My father actually went through life thinking that if he made it to sixty, he would have done well. It wasn't until my great-grandmother died, around the age of ninety-four, that I discovered there was something special about her—something from which none of the others had benefitted. When we researched her life, we found that even though she had never complained about back problems, Great Grandma had gone to the chiropractor—Willie Weisberg—every week, religiously, come Hell or high water. No one understood why but Great Grandma wanted to go, so, she went! Her life was good; she lived to a reasonable old age, her legs swelled up as her kidneys failed during the last six months of her life, and then she was gone.

My brothers and I, who all became chiropractors, realized that Great Grandma was special because she had a nervous system that was functioning properly as a result of what Willie was doing for her. Looking back, I want to kiss Willie for doing such a great job with Great Grandma and I want to strangle him because he, somehow, didn't effectively communicate to her how valuable and important it was to have her family checked and under chiropractic care as well! I judged Willie guilty of "murder by omission" and that incident really changed the focus and direction of my life. When

I reached back, three generations, to Great Grandma and forward, three generations, to my own great-grandchildren, I realized that Willie had a profound effect on my great grandmother but a profound *negative* effect on the rest of the family, through omission. I wanted to do as much good for people as Willie had done but I wanted to do even more by having them understand the value and importance of the entire *family* growing their health rather than just one person in the family growing his or her health.

To a large degree, that's what set me on the road to doing what I've done for the last 35 years. It set me on the road to being a chiropractor and taking care of large numbers of people in the community that I've settled in. It got me focused on inspiring my public through education about what we could do for their lives and health, going forward, rather than what we would do for a problem they may have manifested along the way. After my career reached a certain point, I started coaching other chiropractors with the intention to help them better communicate with their public. I could spread my mission through others who, in turn, could spread that mission in their communities. Ultimately, I developed a chiropractic technique that made it extremely simple for doctors to get the job done in an effective, efficient, and elegant way that left them appropriate time to communicate and educate their patients and their public. This led to the creation of our media company, whose purpose was to get this big idea out and bypass the doctor, who was already full to get the word, the story, the message out to the chiropractor's patients and public.

What has been the hardest part of doing what you do?

The hardest part, lately, is maintaining and growing the vision of the media company and not giving up when other can't see it. I asked myself: *What can I do to get people to embrace something they can't see?* What I realized was that this problem was nothing new. It was something I had to do with my family, my patients, and my community. It was something

I had to do when coaching other chiropractors and it was core when I was teaching a new, different approach to chiropractic technique. Being on the leading edge, being a visionary, and trying to help other people—whether they are professionals or laypeople—embrace that vision... establishing a crystal-clear vision but also sustaining it, maintaining it, and growing it in the face of non-acceptance is always the hardest part.

What keeps you going when things are tough?

A common theme that comes in and keeps me going is thinking of how Willie took the road of least resistance with Great Grandma. He had her under his care. There's no point, really, in explaining anything beyond that. He was happy, he was satisfied, and he was complacent. What keeps me going is that I don't want to be like Willie. However, I *do* want to help folks see a bigger, better future, through inspiration, rather than helping them with desperation. Inspiration, rather than desperation, is the focus of everything I do. People come to chiropractors largely because they're desperate; they've been here, been there, tried this, tried that, and have not found the solutions to their problems. Then the chiropractor helps them with their problems and once the problems go away, the relationships tend to end. What if people were inspired to actually *grow* their health and not just fix their problems? Would their families, their communities, and this society be better off if we were leading through inspiration rather than fixing problems that arose as a result of desperation?

So, what keeps me going? I believe I'm put here to inspire. Not just to help people get rid of problems that they have and don't want but rather to help people create the lives that they want but don't yet have.

What's been the most rewarding part of what you do?

The most rewarding part is the early adopters with the media company. Synergy is the most rewarding piece of the equation; how I can take my one piece and your one piece and potentially make three or more out of them? It's very rewarding when people can embrace your vision and see what their one and your one will produce when they are combined together. The early adopters absolutely keep me going, and are rewarding, even though they are largely outside of chiropractic at this point.

We have a church, in Texas, that wants to communicate with its members, from a spiritual standpoint, using our technology. This is exciting and rewarding and makes me extremely happy! To have an Internet giant, like Alex Mandossian, embrace our technology because he sees how he can take our one and his one and make three out of it, just makes my day. The prize, for me, is that chiropractors are starting to embrace the technology. They see it as an effective vehicle for group coaching and are starting to see it as an effective vehicle for educating their patients and their public.

The reward is that I'm not getting knocked down any more! It's not how many times you get knocked down; it's how many times you get back up. The rewarding part is that we're still on a mission, we're still moving forward, and people are embracing us, and our message, through coaching, techniques, practice, and the media company. When people finally embrace another person's vision, that, in and of itself, is reward.

What is the most inspiring transformation or manifestation that you've witnessed in your work?

I'm inspired most by my children. The vision for the future lies in children and for me, personally, in my children. I'm inspired by the success that my son and daughter-in-law have in their practice. I'm inspired by the success that my daughter has in her practice. They're all being more of who they can be rather than accepting mediocrity. From a moral and ethical standpoint, I look at these three now-adult individuals with not only a parent's pride but a colleague's pride and see that they, too, are making a difference. My son and daughter-in-law are using the technique I developed and now they often seek my counsel. They are growing, they are successful and happy, and they are educating their public and attracting people who want to utilize their services to grow and develop their health rather than just ameliorate their problems. To me, that is complete inspiration and justification to continue doing what I'm doing.

Dr. Bob Levine

"Once people recognize and interrupt their automatic patterns that were restricting change, they are free from the pattern and can then make rapid desired changes."

Dr. Bob Levine recently joined Corporate Wellness Resources, LLC (CWR) as the Director of Wellness and High-Performance Programs. The mission of CWR is to provide programs and opportunities for self-funding institutions to reduce their healthcare costs through improving the health and performance of their people. Dr. Bob is a gifted holistic health practitioner who has pioneered the development and delivery of effective group programs for helping people reduce and eliminate chronic pain, stress, and symptoms of stress-related illnesses. His research-proven programs have been shown to dramatically improve health and human performance.

Dr. Bob's future vision is that all people are optimally healthy and living lives that they love, institutions and people paying for healthcare lower their healthcare costs by more than 75 percent as health improvement drives reduced healthcare utilization, and the money saved in the U.S. economy is used for higher purposes in support of our people.

Dr. Bob received his Ph.D. in Pharmacology from George Washington University in 1982 and has spent over 30 years in basic research on Parkinson's and Alzheimer's diseases, psychiatric illnesses, and aging. He joined Henry Ford Health System (HFHS) in Detroit, Michigan in 1993 after conducting research at the National Institutes of Health and then Wayne State University. He has received numerous federal grants, edited five books, and published over 80 scientific articles. In 2008, he became the Director of the HFHS Center for Integrative Wellness. In 2012, he left Henry Ford to join CWR. He has applied outside-the-box thinking to develop, and take to the next level, unique solutions that help people improve their health and their lives.

To find out more: bob@drboblevine.com or (248) 342-7555

What personal event or universal problem made you want to do what you do?

Until 1994, I was embedded in the conventional medical healthcare model, conducting basic brain research on mechanisms underlying neurological and psychiatric illnesses and premature nerve cell death in aging. I was well funded by grants from the federal government and recognized internationally for my expertise. Until recently, I spent the last 19 years working with Henry Ford Health System in Detroit, Michigan, in various director capacities. With a Ph.D. in pharmacology, I was very clear about the benefits and limitations of pharmaceuticals. In 1993, I finally had both of my knees surgically repaired (ACL reconstructions) after years of aggressive skiing and the resulting ski accidents. These surgeries are representative of some of the best that conventional medical care has to offer, which fall in the categories of restorative surgeries, emergency services, and high-technology diagnoses.

As I have become an expert in accelerated behavioral change, it is clear to me that conventional medicine has failed to reliably produce excellent results in supporting people in making behavioral and lifestyle changes needed to improve, or even eliminate, ill-health conditions. Prime examples are chronic pain and stress-related illnesses. There are many chronic pain conditions, such as back, neck, hip, shoulder, knee, arthritis, and headache, among many others, in which conventional medicine has no definitive strategy to eliminate the pain and improve performance as a result. Managing, rather than eliminating chronic pain has been the primary focus of conventional medical care. Stress is a prominent underlying factor in many ill-health conditions, including chronic pain, sleep disturbance, anxiety, depression, fatigue, high blood pressure, diabetes, and gastrointestinal conditions, among many others. Again, the conventional care approach is to support people in managing stress, rather than interrupting the stress reactions that cause widespread ill-health problems in our society. Most management of pain and stress is accomplished through the use of pharmaceuticals, the main tool of the conventional medical physician. Having studied drug mechanisms for several decades, I have learned that drugs manage symptoms, rather than eliminate the source of an illness. While this can be important in the short-term management of a critical condition, it is best to avoid long-term use of medications, when possible, because of their often potent and damaging side effects. Achieving full symptomatic relief, without the long-term use of pharmaceuticals, should be the goal of every patient and every healthcare professional. This perspective, combined with a personal health challenge in 1994, led me to become a stress and pain elimination expert and help thousands of people get relief from a variety of chronic pain and stress-related conditions.

During 1993 and through 1994, I experienced chronic back and hip pain along with shooting pain (sciatica) down one of my legs. After participating in athletics all of my life, I was reduced to limping around in pain, experiencing reduced performance on the job and in my personal life, gaining weight due to less physical activity, and feeling depressed about my situation. At the age of 40, there was nothing in conventional care that could help me eliminate the pain, and I was told I would need a hip replacement, eventually, and to wait as long as possible so I could outlive the artificial hip. Meanwhile, I was advised to manage the pain with drugs. This was not the future vision of life I had in mind!

In spite of my conventional medical research background and knowing very little about alternative therapies, I elected to pursue alternative therapies that were not covered by my health insurance. I tried over a dozen, in a six-month period, to the tune of two to three hours a week and $6,000 out-of-pocket. It was destiny that I had a long and expensive road to a cure. Finally, I was able to unlock the pain and get back to being active in sports and fully engaged in life. It was quite a revelation! This was life providing me the education I needed to make a difference by helping people struggling with ill-health conditions to improve their health. I realized that the opportunity arose for me to redirect my life and branch out into the area of "holistic" health. While running my basic science research lab, I received training in a variety of techniques, including deep tissue manipulation, acupuncture, hypnosis and other mind-body therapies, and movement education, while treating many individuals with a variety of pain and non-pain conditions with the expertise I was developing. I also trained extensively in effective communication strategies and spent years coaching others to be effective communicators. I now also train others in my specialization of accelerated behavioral change through the proprietary technique of "automatic pattern interruption."

It turns out that all individuals, over their lifetimes, have developed automatic habits and patterns that have restricted their ability to change, and have interfered with producing desired results. Once people recognize and interrupt their automatic patterns that were restricting change, they are free from the pattern and can then make rapid desired changes. Accelerated behavioral change through automatic pattern interruption can be applied to any area of life. I have spent the last 18 years applying this to the universal problem of helping the people of our nation improve their health, so that our society can be free of the constraint of inappropriately high healthcare costs and reduced human performance. Improving health is the only reliable long-term solution to rescuing our corporations, institutions, and other payers of healthcare from the burden of high healthcare costs. It starts with improving each person's health and performance.

Fortunately, my wife, Charlene, has much of the same holistic health training as I have. We started assembling all that we had learned, over the years, from our many teachers and taking all of it to the next level so we could offer our expertise to groups of people who needed help in reducing and eliminating chronic pain, stress, and symptoms of stress-related conditions. We realized the importance of tracking pain elimination, rather than simply looking at pain reduction (management), which is what most of conventional healthcare monitors. Rather than managing pain over time, pain elimination is what we all really want. I was able to bring our expertise to my work at Henry Ford Health System, where, from 2007 to 2012, my team and I offered multi-session group programs, delivered over a few months in clinical studies with employees of several large corporations, including Chrysler, Henry Ford Health System, and Dow Chemical. Through extensively tracking data on the status of pain, stress, sleep disturbance, anxiety, depression, fatigue, work life quality, and other scientifically validated measures, the data proved that participants could make appropriate changes rapidly and achieve relief from a variety of pain and stress-related conditions. In 2011, Blue Cross Blue Shield of Michigan funded the delivery of group programs to some of their patients as well. Over that five year period, the group programs were offered to over 2,500 participants. The clinical data collected showed that nearly 40 percent of all chronic pain conditions were eliminated by the end of the programs and many stress-related conditions helped dramatically, including reductions in sleep disturbance, anxiety, depression, and fatigue, among many others. Long-term use of pharmaceuticals declined as well. The clinical data also showed that the excellent results achieved by participants were generally maintained at least 16 months after the end of the programs. The superlative results from these group programs represent a major breakthrough in caring for people experiencing chronic pain, stress, and symptoms of stress-related conditions. In 2012, I left the Henry Ford Health System and joined Corporate Wellness Resources, LLC, to more rapidly spread this accelerated behavioral change technology throughout our society. By producing a healthier and higher-performing population, healthcare costs to our nation can be dramatically reduced. Helping people improve their health and performance in life, many hundreds to thousands at a time, has become my life's passion.

What has been the hardest part of doing what you do?

It is critical to recognize that things are only hard if we think or say so, or have this perception. One of the critical parts of our group program training is to have people recognize when they are thinking or saying something that would interfere with their ability to produce their desired results in the future. Everyone has a future vision of what they think will happen. When their thinking or speaking is unsupportive of them achieving the results they *really* want, we call that a "corrupt future vision." These unsupportive thoughts and ways of speaking are driven by the unique automatic patterns that all individuals have. We then teach them to be effective at interrupting these automatic patterns. In this way, people are free to develop new and supportive thinking, speaking, and other actions consistent with producing the results they desire in any area of life. (We call this their "true future vision," what they *really* want to happen when they are free to choose).

One of my biggest challenges is dealing with the common perceptions held by most people who have been struggling with ill-health; these include that they think they have tried almost everything, they have failed over and over to improve their health and don't want to fail again, and they simply cannot be helped, even though they understand that my clinical data indicates they have an excellent opportunity to get benefit. These perceptions can keep people from engaging in any potential health improvement activity and keep them stuck where they are. The good news here is that most people realize they are stuck in some automatic pattern without the ability to change, and most would love to find a way out of their pattern so they can achieve rapid behavioral change and produce their desired results. When a person constructs a new future vision free from the limitations of their automatic pattern, they can easily engage in the novel, cost-effective, and ground-breaking programs offered through Corporate Wellness Resources that are designed to reduce and eliminate chronic pain, stress, and symptoms of stress-related illnesses.

A second challenge is that people have not been willing to spend money on their own health, even though they are spending money in ways that are perhaps not as important as their health. There are reasons for this that are easily explained, and we teach that topic in our seminars, which helps with setting priorities. Many people feel that their health insurance should cover all aspects of their care. Conventional health insurance places restrictions on what can be a covered benefit. Even if an alternative approach is proven to be effective, existing restrictions can prevent it from becoming a covered benefit. Furthermore, many people have high co-pays for conventional medical services or high-deductible health plans and are already paying a lot for conventional medical services that may not have resolved their ill-health conditions. If people have their focus on past failures to improve health, they are less likely to adopt a new future vision of improving their health based on their choice to pay out-of-pocket for helpful, novel services. Many Americans are also having to pay more for their healthcare as more and more self-funding institutions and insurance companies are requiring their employees and clients to have a certain level of good health to get the lowest insurance rates (e.g., normal body mass index, non-smoker, low alcohol consumption, normal lipid profile, etc.). Those people who do not meet the measures are forced to pay more in premiums and co-pays. Without providing people the ability to make lifestyle changes that support improved health, we end up with unhappy people who do not feel supported in making changes they need to make to improve health and save money! As an accelerated behavioral change expert, I saw the need to support people in making their desired changes. This led to the group programs, offered by Corporate Wellness Resources, which utilize proven approaches to support accelerated behavioral changes that have people getting the results they desire with health and in many other areas of life!

What keeps you going when things are tough?

I always keep my focus on the true future vision of having all people who participate in Corporate Wellness Resources programs achieve rapid, desired health improvement. When I keep my view on all the people, experiencing ill-health, who are helped by the group programs for relief of chronic pain and stress, the occurrence of anything being "tough" actually disappears. Keeping my future vision on creating a world where all people are optimally healthy and happy in their lives has me excited and inspired to move forward beyond where I might have stopped before; I continue moving forward boldly and take actions consistent with this goal. Things actually occur as tough when the future vision becomes corrupted by feelings of inadequacy and potential failure leading to disappointment. We teach people how to instantly transform a corrupt future vision to their true future vision; they move beyond the feeling that anything is tough. As I maintain my true future vision, I am able to transcend helping one person at a time, to helping many thousands and millions of people, in the shortest period of time, through offering large in-person group programs and unique internet programming. This future vision drives the whole effort. Nothing is "tough" in that true future vision.

What's been the most rewarding part of what you do?

Most rewarding are the novel approaches that Charlene and I, and our team at Corporate Wellness Resources, have created and packaged with existing methods to offer ground-breaking holistic programming that helps people with a wide variety of chronic pain and stress-related illnesses, which are often quite serious and costly. Our programs help participants make rapid, desired, and meaningful changes in areas of life where they had previously been constrained. The fact that we help so many people, with a wide variety of conditions, in the same group program is also satisfying, knowing that nearly everyone gets help in ways that are meaningful to them. It is so gratifying to be on the leading edge of the movement that is going to help many millions of people improve health and be free to live the lives they have always wanted, all while reducing the cost of healthcare for individuals and institutions. In addition to the data we track to prove program effectiveness, we receive so many amazing testimonials of how people have been helped by the program. The testimonials come from the hearts of our participants and their gratitude is palpable. That is rewarding.

What is the most inspiring transformation or manifestation that you've witnessed in your work?

Having offered treatment and group programs to many thousands of people over the years, there are so many instances of people being helped in remarkable and sometimes unexpected ways. A person had quit running marathons due to severe chronic back pain and, after attending, started running marathons again at the age of over 60. A person with restless legs syndrome completely eliminated the condition during participation. Someone, who had not slept well for decades, transformed into a great sleeper. In fact, sleep disturbance disappears quickly for most. Migraine and other chronic headaches have disappeared in many participants. Medications of all types have been reduced and eliminated, from pain medication to drugs for high blood pressure, diabetes, anxiety, depression, and many other stress-related conditions. Perhaps the biggest overall benefit to our participants is the growth in confidence that replaces the resignation that is driven automatically: confidence in their ability to eliminate chronic pain and symptoms of their stress-related conditions, confidence in their ability to perform at a higher level, and confidence in their ability to support others in achieving results that everyone wants. While our programs deliver relief of pain and stress-related illnesses as a prime vehicle for saving money on healthcare expenditures, knowing that we impact people, as a whole, and inspire their transformation in ways that they do not expect, yet appreciate, is most inspiring!

Charles Poliquin

"I'm a big believer in changing one, or maybe two things per week, and that's it."

Charles Poliquin is recognized as one of the most successful strength coaches in the world. A native of Ottawa, Canada, Charles completed graduate studies in Exercise Physiology and began coaching elite athletes at a young age. He has spent years researching European journals (he is fluent in English, French, and German) and speaking to other coaches and scientists in his quest to optimize training methods.

With the influence of his coaching, Charles' athletes have achieved hundreds of medals, wins, and personal bests. He has coached athletes at Olympics since 1984 and is known worldwide for producing faster athletes. When a country wants a gold medal, they come to Charles. Charles has had Olympic medalists in seventeen different sports and world record holders in ten sports.

Charles has perfected the art of combining nutrition with training routines that produce results, and his books and courses are the culmination of his theories and knowledge. He has published thirteen books including the popular *German Body Comp Program*, which provides a complete diet and fitness program that anyone can use to achieve the optimal body composition.

Charles' interest in achieving the best nutrition for a healthy lifestyle and optimal performance led him to develop the BioSignature Modulation program, which uses a body composition assessment to guide dietary protocols. He turned this program, which has served his clients so well, into the BioSignature Certification in order to share his knowledge and practice with the rest of the world.

To find out more: www.CharlesPoliquin.com

What personal event or universal problem made you want to do what you do?

I started off as a strength coach and was producing Olympic medalists on a regular basis. I've had Olympic medalists in 17 different sports and world record holders in 10 sports. I was writing for different publications and being interviewed by different publications and the most commonly asked question was, "If I am a common person, can you still help me?" Of course, humans are humans; we have basically the same genes, so good advice and scientific advice always helps anybody. I started to have a website in 2001, which helped propagate the message I had to share. Initially, there were basically meatheads and athletes coming to the site, and progressively we had a larger proportion of females and older people who came in. The spectrum and readership changed dramatically over the last two years, so much that we had to start a separate website, the Poliquin Lifestyle website, which tends to cater more to the female population because the male is not so into hard-core, busy changes.

It was amazing to me that the average person follows what I call "politically correct" advice, which is disastrous to results. In other words, most of the advice preached in the media is slanted by a different lobby and also by people repeating antiquated concepts. For example, people still believe that doing aerobic work is the best way to lose fat. Well, it is one of the worst things you can do for yourself; it ages your brain prematurely, amongst other things.

My mission is to propagate healthy, scientific advice so people can achieve their results in body, mind, and spirit. For example, a lot of people go to gyms and they exercise on the electronic equipment. Well, electronic equipment actually increases the rate at which you become insulin resistant—by about 46 percent. In other words, if you do aerobic training on a treadmill, you're basically training to become a diabetic. This is found in the scientific literature, so I keep people updated with that stuff.

Obviously, the food industry lobbies a lot and most of our food recommendations, by our beloved government, come from lobbying and not from science. So, for example, the grain industry has a very strong influence on how we're told we're supposed to eat, but it's actually disastrous to our health; it basically helps propagate diabetes in our country.

My mission is to get people the right information. And, it's free, so you can't argue with free; it's the best price. We're translated in 20 languages, and we've certified coaches in 68 countries. The big result of that is, obviously, it helps my credibility and it helped me open a lot of doors worldwide, but we actually have 20 volunteers who translate the information into 20 different languages, and that number keeps growing. These are not Google translations; these are real, native speakers' translations of my articles. In December 2009, I had 30,000 visitors a month to my website. As of this month, we're going to hit 600,000, so that's 20 times more people, since December 2009, who have come to my website on a monthly basis to get the free information.

What has been the hardest part of doing what you do?

The hardest part is battling the politically correct information, which is actually false. I have to undo work. If you don't know something, and you have no idea, it's pretty easy to shape your mind, but I'm battling years and years of propaganda. For example, the whole cholesterol thing is a myth. It's not a very good heart disease predictor; there are far better things you can look at, like a compliance of arteries and so on. That's information we try to propagate throughout the general population.

I don't find it hard. I find it a challenge, but you will find that some countries are more engrained in their policies, especially countries where the ultimate authority, after God, is medical doctors. So, for example, in Denmark, the Danish population is very influenced by the medical community. The problem is that the medical community is about 40 years outdated. That's the bigger challenge in that country, compared to in the U.S., where the information is current and more readily available. I find that the battles are more geographically determined than anything else.

What keeps you going when things are tough?

When you're passionate about something, if you start looking at obstacles, keep sight of the goal in mind. I do run into obstacles, like anyone else, otherwise it would not be a challenge, but I'm very passionate about what I do. I want people to know what's best for them. One of the best tools for that is Janet Attwood's book, *The Passion Test*. I read my passions every day, and one of them is to be a world-class leader. So, when I'm confronted with decisions, I'll always go back to: *Is this in line with my passions? Yes or no?* If it is in line, then I do it; if it's not, then I don't do it. It's a very simple system, but simple does not mean it's not effective. I come from a martial arts background, and usually the simplest techniques are the most effective ones.

What's been the most rewarding part of what you do?

Actually, the most rewarding part is the daily emails we get. For example, I got this email from an 88-year-old lady from Florida, and her doctor wanted to put her on Lipitor®. This woman is very well-educated. She searched on the Internet and saw all the side-effects she could get from using statins. Very few people know that there are 150,000 cases a year of transient global amnesia in the U.S. alone. That means some people wake up one day and they don't know who they are, they can't recognize their spouse or their kids, and that's induced by statins—that's one of the side effects. I'm not talking about all the damage to muscles and so on.

So, this lady read my articles and she told her doctor, "Can I have a month on my own before you put me on the statins? I want to try something." All she did was use the herbal preparation curcumin, which is also known as turmeric, so it's an Indian herb. Turmeric, or curcumin, actually lowers oxidized forms of LDL. LDL is quickly named the "bad cholesterol" but there are actually good forms of it and bad forms of it. Curcumin, because it reduces inflammation in the body, reduces oxidized LDL, which is the bad one.

This lady complied perfectly with her lipid profile in 25 days, and the doctor said, "Well, you don't have to go on statins. You proved your point." She had an open-minded doctor.

When I get an email like that, then I know I'm doing something right— and I get emails like that every day. Sometimes it's a child, whose mother writes to me and says, "My child was autistic, and we followed your dietary recommendations and my child is much better behaved, learns faster, and has better coordination." The same way a fortune is built a penny at a time, I think transforming people's concept, and also *owning* their health, is something done one person at a time. The good news is that I get more and more of those emails. I had 2,000 fans on Facebook a few years ago, and now I have 30,000 fans. Obviously the word is getting around, and on Facebook we provide free information every day. To have seen the numbers grow is very rewarding, but it's a daily thing.

What is the most inspiring transformation or manifestation that you've witnessed in your work?

My lawyer was morbidly obese and had sleep apnea. He was a walking heart attack and he weighed 407 pounds. The first month, I made him gain 29 pounds of muscle but lose 31 pounds of fat. Eighteen months later, he was 155 pounds, and he's kept that weight since 2003. Basically, he lost two persons! I think that's a pretty awesome transformation.

The thing I do, that's probably different from most people, is that I don't run a cult. I'm a big believer in changing one, or maybe two things per week, and that's it. I don't ask for a lot of commitment, I ask for a consistently increasing commitment, but not to the point where you're obsessive. For example, it could be as simple as the types of shampoos and moisturizers you use. We have a website that we refer people to, and it's free: www.ewg.org. They analyze all cosmetics throughout the world and give them a rating depending on how toxic they are. Sometimes, someone can't lose weight just because of the shampoo or moisturizer they use. For example, there is one type of moisturizer, widely sold in the U.S., which contains five types of xenoestrogens. They're chemicals that resemble estrogens, but without the good benefits; they only have the side effects of estrogen. When you absorb five different ones of those molecules every day, you're basically castrating yourself and over-feminizing yourself. So, for a male who uses a moisturizer, you might as well put his testicles in a microwave; it does pretty much the same thing. Once you become aware that it's as simple as their moisturizer and remove it from their daily routine, suddenly their body fat drops! It wasn't much of a change as far as commitment or mental effort, just a switch from one to the other, and—boom!—fat loss. All xenoestrogens accelerate cancer growth. There's a direct correlation between xeno, or foreign, estrogens in your body and the rate at which you deal with cancer. So, just removing unhealthy stuff from your daily hygiene habits can make a huge difference!

Dr. Woody Beck

"Neurological rehabilitation is a new and innovative way to quickly and safely upregulate the nervous system. This, in itself, is a stand-alone treatment for any neurologic condition."

For over 38 years, W.W. Beck, DC, QN (also known as Dr. Woody Beck) has been in service to his community. Dr. Beck has been a featured speaker throughout North Carolina, and has taught many seminars about the benefits of chiropractic and how to have a healthier life. He and his wife have been married for 42 years, they have two grown children who are married to chiropractors, and they have three grandchildren. Dr. Beck is the author of the much-anticipated book, *The 21st Century Chiropractic*.

To find out more: www.BeckAndBlackleyChiro.com & beckchiropractic@bellsouth.net

What personal event or universal problem made you want to do what you do?

What's a man to do? I had just served my tour in the U.S. Army, I was 21 years old, going to college, and—whoops—I injured my back. I went to a medical doctor and, sadly, received no help. My dad suggested I go to a chiropractor. At that time in my life, I didn't have a clue about what a chiropractor was. However, I went and got amazing results. The doctor took a liking to me and encouraged me to consider going—even challenged me to go—to chiropractic college. A few months later, I was accepted and enrolled at Palmer College of Chiropractic in Davenport, Iowa. Now I have been practicing chiropractic in Lumberton, North Carolina for 38 years. It's amazing how a back injury can change your whole life in such a positive manner—a great example of making lemonade out of lemons.

What has been the hardest part of doing what you do?

By far, the most difficult part of being a chiropractor is trying to explain how chiropractic works, and how it is going to have a positive effect on my patients' health. This situation is further complicated because all patients want instant relief, in our over-medicated world. I try to explain how chiropractic care helps us to live a more pain free and healthy lifestyle without the use of drugs.

What keeps you going when things are tough?

Of course, life itself can be a challenge; it has its ups and downs. My dad used to say, "When the going gets tough, the tough get going," and I've found that to be true; it's a time to dig in and apply yourself. However, I believe a strong faith in God has given me strength, which has allowed me to have the self-confidence to deal with difficult situations as they arose.

What's been the most rewarding part of what you do?

Being a chiropractor is a blessing to me because I truly enjoy helping people feel better. It doesn't matter whether I am treating an infant with colic, an elderly person who can't raise their arm, a person suffering with a migraine, or a simple neck pain; I am always thrilled and humbled when my patients respond favorably.

What is the most inspiring transformation or manifestation that you've witnessed in your work?

Without a doubt, the most exciting transformation in my practice was when I began to treat my patients with Quantum Neurology®. Quantum Neurology®, along with laser therapy, allows the doctor to do neurological rehabilitation.

Neurological rehabilitation is a new and innovative way to quickly and safely upregulate the nervous system. This, in itself, is a stand-alone treatment for any neurologic condition.

Being a Quantum Neurologist™ has allowed me the privilege and opportunity to treat many chronic and severe neurologic cases. I feel that neurological rehabilitation is a great gift to humanity and definitely is a miraculous treatment.

Lisa M. Collins

"The most rewarding part is when someone comes and tells me that I've inspired them or I've helped to change their life... when they say 'thank you' and there are tears in their eyes."

Lisa M. Collins lives in the beautiful state of New Mexico, where she was born and raised. Lisa has three amazing children and, for the last 18 years, she has been married to her soul mate, Randy. They are blessed with an abundance of family around them. Lisa says, "I thank God, every morning when I awaken, for the many blessings and for our home-based business that changed our lives and introduced us to personal development."

Lisa and Randy were introduced to Xango seven years ago, after Lisa got a career-threatening illness. They had amazing results with the products and both became pain free. They never had a desire to work the business until Lisa lost two of her three jobs. They were handed some tools and off to work they went with Xango.

What Lisa loves most, about her business, is all the people she's had a chance to connect with and assist. Once Lisa and Randy started working the business, they did in 18 months what took Lisa 23 years as a hairdresser to do. That has allowed her and Randy to *live again* and *dream*!

To find out more: www.DreamBuilders.MyMangosteen.com & rnldream@msn.com & (505) 486-5508 (Lisa) & (505) 486-0258 (Randy)

What personal event or universal problem made you want to do what you do?

I was conceived from an affair and placed for adoption. I was raised by my biological mother's sister. My mom did a wonderful job raising me as an only child. Then there was a turn of events. I got pregnant at the age of 14 and my amazing daughter was born. When I was 17 and my daughter, Mandy, was only a year-and-a-half old, her daddy was killed in a motorcycle accident. I felt very alone, as a child and a single mother, caring for a baby; thank God for my fantastic parents. I pulled myself together and enrolled in beauty school after I received my G.E.D. at the age of 18.

I remember sitting in the break room one day, crying over the loss of my boyfriend who had passed, and my friend said, "I want to help you, so come to lunch with me." We arrived at her house and were sitting in the kitchen. She opened up a cabinet, pulled out a tray, and said, "This is cocaine. It will make you feel better." At that very moment, I was hooked.

The year that followed was Hell. My parents admitted me into rehab with a $200 per week cocaine habit at the age of 19. I weighed just a little less than 90 pounds. I got out of rehab and relapsed a few times. Then, I remember driving home one day and it was dark the sky was completely grey because there was a big storm coming in, and it was super gloomy. I looked in my rear-view mirror and, behind me, the sky was clear and blue. That was my "aha" moment, when I realized where I was going instead of where I needed to be. So, that night, I, literally, packed up my trailer and moved back home with my parents.

I always felt that people saw me as a loser. I felt abandoned and that I would never amount to anything. I felt like I had failed everyone. Then, one day, I woke up and said, "I will be a household name!"

What has been the hardest part of doing what you do?

The hardest part has been sharing with people that there are no limitations in their lives, trying to convey that and encouraging them to push the "reset" button. I still have a job that I love, that I choose to go to, but I *love* being at home working with people and working with my business that I have here. I think the hardest part is not having the ability to connect with more people, which I would like to do.

What keeps you going when things are tough?

What keeps me going is my spirituality—remembering that I am a miracle and I was placed here to do something amazing. I get fueled by other people's stories, or a team member that I've helped, or somebody that comes back and says a simple "thank you."

What's been the most rewarding part of what you do?

The most rewarding part is when someone comes and tells me that I've inspired them or I've helped to change their life…when they say "thank you" and there are tears in their eyes.

What is the most inspiring transformation or manifestation that you've witnessed in your work?

For me, the most inspiring things are personal growth and releasing old patterns, but the greatest part of all is watching others have growth in their own lives and businesses, and hearing their success stories. I helped a couple with one of the products that we sell. The woman had a disease and had not left the house in over five years. After being on the products for four to five months, the couple went on their very first vacation!

Ari Gronich

*"Having a career in the healing arts is, in and of itself,
a path of self-transformation."*

Ari Gronich is a Sports Therapist, Injury Rehabilitation and Prevention Specialist, Sports Hypnotherapist, Reiki Master, Speaker, and a Corporate Wellness Provider. While exploring sports therapy with a major pro sports team, he learned from some of the top therapists, doctors, and trainers in the business, giving him one of the most well-rounded and expansive training bases and knowledge bases in the industry, with over 5,000 hours of training, gaining certificate after certificate in a great multitude of modalities.

Ari attended life-transforming workshops, such as EST at age eight, and Lifespring, Summit, and the Forum, all before he was a teenager. He practiced Buddhism alongside going to temple studying for his Bar Mitzvah, and then his self-inquiring mind brought him to studying other religions, philosophies, and spiritual paths.

Ari has presented workshops with Mark Victor Hansen, Robert Allen and the Enlightened Wealth Institute, Clinton Swaine, T. Harv Eker, and many others.

As a healer, Ari brings love, experience, strength, and compassion. He brings a sense of peace and understanding that you won't find in just anyone, and a deep understanding that nothing needs to be fixed in you. You are perfect and whole just as you are. Every session is holistic and personal. Ari takes styles from all over the world and combines them in a unique way that is solely about your healing. It is all about *you*, not a technique or specific modality, but a channeled, spiritually guided journey into you.

To find out more: www.PerformanceTherapist.com & www.AchieveHealthUSA.com & (310) 363-0FIT (0348)

What personal event or universal problem made you want to do what you do?

There are so many events leading up to my journey to becoming a sports therapist. I was an athlete, growing up, and I participated in a lot of physical activities, including tennis from age three, baseball for eight years, I was a gymnast for eight years, I did long-distance cycling, and martial arts. I was always in the athletic realm. One of the problems was that as children we weren't taught about injury prevention. We weren't taught about stretching or performance enhancement. We were just taught, "Play your sport. If you play your sport, you'll get better at it." Therefore, I would get injured on a fairly regular basis.

I started going to my first chiropractor when I was five years old. I was cramping, getting injured, and my shoulders were going out. I was seeking places where I could recover from the pain. The only performance enhancers that we knew about back then were steroids. I don't know if you remember Lyle Alzado, but he was a football legend who got sick and died of brain cancer brought on by steroid use. That was the big performance enhancement thing. It wasn't about how you trained or how you worked your core. It wasn't about any of those things. What got me involved was all of the pain I was in and wanting to perform at a higher level but not knowing what that meant.

What has been the hardest part of doing what you do?

I would say that communication is the hardest part. How do you communicate to somebody who's never felt a certain way what their potential is if they were to train with you? What's the difference in five-tenths of a second? With an elite athlete, it's a little easier because they know what the difference is. They know that their bodies go through a huge transformation between 11 seconds and 10.5 seconds. There's a huge difference in how you feel in your body, but how do you translate that potential to somebody who isn't an athlete? People will come to see me because they're in pain. But how do I translate the performance enhancement or the injury prevention? It's something that hasn't happened yet.

One of the hardest parts is that there are so many people in the industry—the massage industry and so forth—who have very little training and don't do what I do. So, somebody goes to a massage therapist but there can be so many things they don't know. Once I get them onto the table, it's much easier because I have a huge passion for it. How do I communicate the quality, the difference, before they ever come see me? It's so hard to communicate that.

What keeps you going when things are tough?

What keeps me going is my sense of purpose! I think that I was brought here, I was given a gift, and having that sense of purpose is what keeps me going when things are tough. I know that God has given me a tremendous ability to heal. I've been told I have "hands of gold," that my hands are incredible. I've had so many people come to me after going to chiropractors, therapists, and so many other professionals for massage and physical therapy. Then they come to me and they say, "Man, you have amazing hands! I've never felt anything quite like this!" I have the belief and the knowledge—but mostly the faith—that I'm here for a reason. I haven't completed that purpose yet, and I have to keep going.

What's been the most rewarding part of what you do?

It's seeing people's faces when they arrive in pain, they're distraught, and they've been to all kinds of other therapists and people—then they see me and I'm able to wash away that pain, wash away their fears, wash away the anxiety and the not-knowing of where this is all coming from and why it's here. Watching their faces light up at the end of a treatment is probably the most rewarding part of what I do.

I was so blessed to have a particular client come to me about thirteen years ago. He had been paralyzed for thirty years. For the first ten, he was a quadriplegic, and the last twenty he was a paraplegic. He had been to some of the top specialists in the world at Cedars-Sinai and UCLA. He came in to see me, and for some reason I just looked at his body a little differently. Within three months, I had him walking! He was walking every day, he could move his legs forward, and he could feel my fingers on his toes for the first time in thirty years. How rewarding, for me, to be a catalyst for somebody who had that much pain and that much not-knowing, and then to have such relief and change—after thirty years. Having anything change was a positive benefit! That's probably the most rewarding thing that I've done.

What is the most inspiring transformation or manifestation that you've witnessed in your work?

The one I just mentioned would be the most inspiring transformation. I had a pro tennis player come to me recently with a knee injury that he'd had for seven-plus years, and in ten minutes I cleared up the knee injury completely. That was almost nine months ago, and it hasn't come back. I've had several occurrences like that, throughout my career, where somebody's been in pain for many years, gone to specialists, and in a few minutes, I'm able to clear up that kind of damage. That's been the most inspiring manifestation.

The second inspiring manifestation was being in Athens during the 2004 Paralympics, training a team of about thirty Greek therapists and having a team of fifty therapists from eighteen countries…being one of the team captains and getting to witness all of the world records, and all of the gold medals, and the inspiring athletes who do athletics as a way of living. In some of their countries, they're literally ostracized out of their communities, so the only way they get to live is by competing in these games. I think that was probably the most heartfelt, touching month of my career.

Having a career in the healing arts is, in and of itself, a path of self-transformation. By being in this field, I have grown as a person in ways that I could never have imagined. I am so honored to have accepted the faith and gift to have walked this path.

Diana Lees & Alan Little

"When the light goes on with people and they start taking care of themselves and changing their body balance so they change their physiological situation, we've seen how it can improve their lives."

Diana Lees is an emerging authority in alternative health with a focus on solutions for stress and anxiety. Her background combines a traditional education in Biology plus 25 years in pharma/biotech research, followed by 10 years immersed in alternative medicine. When she discovered she was suffering from Long-Term Stress, her life changed. Mentored and influenced by thought leaders in Naturopathy and Energy Medicine— and living in this crazy time—she understands Long-Term Stress both scientifically and personally, and believes that stress is the most deadly health threat humanity is facing today…but only if we ignore it! Everyone has the power to reverse its deadly effects and it is Diana's mission to bring this message to the world. She founded TotallyVital.com with her husband, Alan Little, to do that.

Alan Little has a diverse background in business, technology, and marketing. His technical projects are powered by a focus on customers and he is committed to building systems that people need, want, and use. He is passionate about health, nutrition, and the planet. When his mother suffered an unexpected decline after receiving a "safe" prescription drug, Alan started questioning and learning.

When he first tried the TotallyVital products, he got excited; they were relatively unknown, and had huge potential to help others. He founded TotallyVital with Diana Lees to bring them to the attention of a wide audience. His mission is to raise awareness about how Long-Term Stress affects humanity today, and he is committed to reaching thousands, even millions, of people with that message and solutions for a better life.

To find out more: www.TotallyVital.com & diana@totallyvital.com

What personal event or universal problem made you want to do what you do?

Diana:

I would have to call it an epiphany that snuck up on me. Last summer—the summer of 2011—I saw myself in the answers to some questions. It was a mind-blowing realization. The questions were on an intake questionnaire for a naturopathic doctor we work with, Dr. Borkin, and they were designed to determine if the person had this condition called Long-Term Stress. We *all* live under stress, right? Stress is what we live with, what we breathe, so it never really dawned on me that there would be this actual, medically recognized, physical condition called Long-Term Stress. If you've been under stress for too long, it doesn't matter whether you meditate, use EFT Tapping, or take a long vacation; there's a point at which your body hits a tipping point, and a chain reaction actually begins where the body can't stop by itself. I saw myself in the questions about symptoms that the body has after the tipping point. The more severe the symptoms, the more severe the condition, the longer you've had it. Well, I was in the red zone, the danger zone. I was at the very edge of, "You're about to go into adrenal exhaustion," where the adrenal glands just give up on you. I had no idea, and I'd had these symptoms my whole life.

Honestly, when I started working with this naturopath, our idea was to bring his products out to the public, because they're really beautiful products. I did not understand, yet, the power of stress and what it does in the body. I hadn't had recent trauma; I'd had these symptoms since I was in my childhood and teens, so I grew up with them, but many people don't get these symptoms until they're older. When I saw myself, I thought: *Holy Maloney! I've got to do something different here.* So, I started using the product Dr. Borkin has for this specific issue because Long-Term Stress is also the doorway to other diseases. In 2005, the American Medical Association named stress the number one proxy killer—the underlying cause of 80 to 85 percent of all fatal diseases. Those diseases include cancer, diabetes, heart disease, Alzheimer's, and other long-term and chronic things like depression, bi-polar, OCD, ADD, ADHD, and autism, some of which are neurological. So, this physiological chain-reaction, if you want to call it that, can really open the door to stuff that's hiding in your genes that you might not have had to deal with.

Our goal is to get that word out so people understand they don't necessarily have to be a victim of their family genetic history, and they don't have to be a victim of stress.

Alan:

A lot of people think: *Oh well, I've lived with this my whole life, so what's the big deal?* Well, it will eventually kill you through one of the diseases Diana mentioned. Even if you don't believe it, look at what's showing up in the children. Since 9/11 happened, which put the whole nation under extreme fear, uncertainty, and doubt with draconian laws, America went from feeling invulnerable, winning every war, to: *My God, somebody could just take a plane and crash it into a building and kill thousands of people.* The Long-Term Stress has hockey-sticked. It's showing up in the epidemic of ASD (Autism Syndrome Disorder), which includes ADD, ADHD, Autism, and Asperger's. It's showing up in our children, so you might not care about it as an adult, but do you care about your kids? There's a direct correlation. Who had heard of this 20 years ago? It was unknown. When I was a kid, I don't remember kids having ADD, so there's a direct correlation here. It's really because the mother is stressed. When the mother is under stress, there's a physiological chain-reaction and there's hormone robbing going on. So, the mother, unknowingly, is robbing hormones from the kids and the kids are born with a hormone imbalance. There's a main underlying cause and a lot of evidence that links ASD with hormone imbalance.

When I was younger, I worked in an institution for kids. These developmental disabilities didn't exist back then, or they weren't spoken about back then, but there were kids with other disabilities, and they were warehoused—they were drugged out of existence, locked away. They might as well have been prisoners. It touched me very deeply, so this is something I care a lot about. My plea to people is, even if you don't care about your own life, please think about your children.

What has been the hardest part of doing what you do?

Diana:

Sometimes, we both feel like a voice in the wilderness, because people just don't know what they don't know. The signs are all there, the evidence is there, but mainstream thinking and mainstream media don't connect the dots. Western medicine only deals with the downstream effects.

Symptoms of Long-Term Stress are things like getting dizzy when you stand up quickly, or having trouble going to sleep, staying asleep, or waking up in the morning, crying really easily for no apparent reason, or even being a little depressed. If you have trouble with your blood pressure when you stand up quickly, Western medicine likes to treat it with blood pressure medication. Well, it can be a symptom of a hormone imbalance. If you can't sleep, they like to give you sleeping aids. Well, that's also a symptom of a hormone imbalance. If you are liable to cry quickly, they think you're depressed. If you're acting depressed or anxious, they want to give you a drug for that. Those can be symptoms of the same hormone imbalance in the body. So, we have a lot of education to do. We have to help people understand and connect the dots.

Alan:

There's so much misinformation out there about stress. Stress, with a small "s," is talked about all the time, which is why we call the physiological chain-reaction Long-Term Stress. This is not about the jerk who cut you off in traffic or having a bad day at work. This is about something that's going on in your body that's like a nuclear reactor going critical. People think: *Oh, stress, oh well! I'll just tap it away, or I'll just take a long vacation, or go to a spa.* I call that slapping a Band-Aid® on a bullet hole, because if you've got Long-Term Stress, this stuff might help you feel better in the moment, but it doesn't do diddly-squat to stop the physiological chain-reaction. The challenge, here, is getting this message out when there is so much misinformation. It's connecting the dots for people and showing them that a whole lot of stuff that sounds unrelated is actually related. So, that's both our challenge and our opportunity.

What keeps you going when things are tough?

Diana:

Well, there are a couple of answers to that, but the more forward-thinking one is, basically, that we're staring at a smoking gun. We understand the whole picture in a way that few people do. When the light goes on with people and they start taking care of themselves and changing their body balance so they change their physiological situation, we've seen how it can improve their lives. So we both have a desire to get the word out and to see more and more people experience these beautiful shifts and healing.

Alan:

There's actually some evidence that infant mortality rates are starting to backslide; we're actually going backwards with that. There's some pretty gritty stuff happening out there. It's easy to want to ignore it, but facts are facts. So we want to do this, not by slamming people over the head with it, but just pointing out the relationships. We want people to know, but we want to do it in a loving, empowering way, without creating more fear. We're definitely not about using fear to sell anything, or piling on any more fear. We don't want to sell anti-stress medications by causing people to feel more stressed out.

What's been the most rewarding part of what you do?

Diana:

As the one on our team who does most of the customer-facing and people-facing activities, it has been phenomenal for me to witness the light going on for people, and the hope that they suddenly have. Most people who have had these symptoms for a while have wondered what the h-e-double-hockey-sticks was going on. They've been trying to find solutions but haven't found them. So I ask a few questions about their symptoms, and I say, "Well, do you have this, this, and this?" They respond, "How did you know?" and their feeling that—*oh, my gosh, there's a solution. Somebody can help me find a solution*—is hugely rewarding. The longer process, of course, is that solution taking effect. It's not a magic bullet, like, "Swallow this potion and you'll be instantly better!" But if people take their time, work with the products to support their bodies, and work to change their life patterns to support their stress levels, and they begin to come back into real balance, it's a beautiful thing to witness!

What is the most inspiring transformation or manifestation that you've witnessed in your work?

Diana:

There's a beautiful story of a woman, called Vivian, who came to me about six or eight months ago, in the middle of last winter.

When she walked in, she said, "I have *no* energy. I can barely get myself out of bed in the morning, I'm constantly exhausted, I can barely think straight, and I'm anxious all the time."

We ran through the questions I mentioned previously, and it was obvious that she needed support. She had a very clear case of Long-Term Stress. I am neither a practitioner, nor a diagnostician, but evidence is evidence.

She started using products to support her adrenal glands (to interrupt that physiological chain reaction), support her thyroid (to give her a little more energy), support her brain (to give her a little more clarity so she could think more clearly), and to calm her emotions so she wasn't constantly anxious. There was a very quick response. Within about two or three weeks, I ran into her, locally, and she was on top of the world.

She said, "Oh my God, I have not felt this good in 20 years!"

That was a beautiful window into what was possible. Of course, it's a balance. If a bicycle goes off balance when you're putting it back in balance, you don't just slam it into a middle position. You follow the process to bring the body back into balance in a similar way. She had hit the balance perfectly that day. But it doesn't necessarily stay that way forever, just because you hit it that particular day. So, she's been going through this process over the last six to eight months, and it's been interesting for her. When she walked into our house to check out these products, she wasn't thinking clearly. That's one of the symptoms of Long-Term Stress, because the frontal lobes don't really work well when your body is in Long-Term Stress. It's really hard to follow directions when you can't think clearly, so she couldn't stay in balance right away.

But she did her best and kept at it, and kept checking in with me and asking, "What do I do now?"

About four months later, all of a sudden, she said, "You know what? I don't need to use the mood calmer; I'm not anxious anymore! And—wait a minute—I'm thinking again!"

Some of the other physical symptoms were still there, but she was much more optimistic. Not long after that, her childhood sweetheart reappeared, they kindled a romance, and a few months later, they started to talk about getting married. It's a powerful transformation to watch a woman come from exhaustion, and really being at the end of her rope, to not only having rejuvenated energy and power, and bringing her body back into balance, but also rejuvenating her reason to live. It's beautiful.

Alan:

When this woman showed up, she said she felt like her brain was a fried egg and she couldn't get out of bed in the morning. She had no energy, was working at a job she hated, and had nobody in her life. She went from quitting that job she hated, to having that boyfriend, having a life, and being a fully-functioning human being. That's what we live for. That's awesome.

Diana:

I want to add something important. The symptoms of Long-Term Stress are really simple, straightforward symptoms that, taken together, mean there's stuff going on in the body. Most people have some of them. They don't become a real problem until you've had a lot of them for a fairly good amount of time. That's when you start getting into the danger zone. That's where I was when I learned about this. So we really want to catch people's awareness *before the problems develop* because there are such simple ways to rebalance and support the body. It does not require you make drastic changes. We're all trained to think: *I get sick, then I go to the doctor.* But what we're saying is, if you *do* take care of yourself now, because you're catching the little niggles of these symptoms now, you don't have to go to the doctor later. It's much easier, it's much more graceful, and it's much simpler in your life. Why go through the trauma and the strain of cancer, heart disease, or Alzheimer's if you don't have to?

Diana Di Gioia

"We've created a place where many people can receive so much in such a simple a way, and then made the door wide enough that a really diverse group of people can get in."

Diana Di Gioia is a licensed acupuncturist, an experienced clinician, teacher, and activist for affordable acupuncture. Her clinic, Community Acupuncture on Cape Cod, in Dennis, Massachusetts, was among the first in the country to offer this revolutionary practice model that focuses on affordability and social justice. She is a graduate of New England School of Acupuncture and has been in practice since 1995.

Diana is also a singer-songwriter, and has released two CDs with her duo, Out Late. Her songs are varied in topic and style, dipping into a range of roots genres and written with a diverse audience in mind. At their core, they are heartfelt stories of love, life, and authenticity, full of courage and free of inhibitions.

To find out more: www.AcuForAll.com & www.ReverbNation.com/OutLateWithDianaDiGioia

What personal event or universal problem made you want to do what you do?

The problem was a lack of access to acupuncture for people of modest or average means. I had spent 10 years doing private room acupuncture and seen that the vast number of people couldn't afford to come enough to get a result, or couldn't afford to come at all. That led to a lot of frustration because I couldn't be effective, and it also led me to feel morally out of sync because I do believe that health care is a right, not a privilege, and yet I wasn't figuring out how to make it something that most people would be able to have access to.

What has been the hardest part of doing what you do?

There's a lot that's hard. Running a small business, alone, with just enough profit margin to pay me a living wage, is hard. Finding other acupuncturists to hire—which is something I'm looking to do now—is hard, because the cost of education is way too high compared to what people can earn working in the field.

What keeps you going when things are tough?

Definitely my spouse, Melody, keeps me going. She really believes in what I do, and believes in me, and that is a huge support.

I have a lot of comrades in the People's Organization of Community Acupuncture. They definitely keep my going because they are running this thing like open source software. When they get a good idea, they share it. When they have experiences that work out in how to run their clinics, they share them. When people have trouble, they help problem solve. So, I'm definitely not alone, even though I said running a small business was the hardest part. I'm alone physically, here in my office, but I'm not alone nationally, and I'm not alone with my problems. I have a lot of support.

My patients also keep me going. They are so obviously benefitting and they so obviously don't have a lot of options that could give them what Community Acupuncture gives them.

What's been the most rewarding part of what you do?

Definitely helping people who otherwise wouldn't get help is the biggest part. Seeing that people can now have enough acupuncture to get a result makes me feel so much more effective. When I was doing private room acupuncture for a higher price tag, most people came half as frequently as they needed to and were therefore getting a fraction of the results they could get. Now, I really feel like I'm putting my training to the fullest use. Feeling *useful* is huge. I treat a lot of people and they get better, they feel better, and I help them. I feel really useful.

The other thing that is rewarding is seeing folks, resting and healing side-by-side, who are divided in so many ways in our culture. They're divided by class, race, age, and religion, and yet here they are in my treatment room, in these recliners, looking like they're just taking naps in a big old living room, side-by-side. I love that!

What is the most inspiring transformation or manifestation that you've witnessed in your work?

I think the most important transformation and manifestation I've seen is not in a person; I think it's within the clinic itself. We've created a place where many people can receive so much in such a simple a way, and then made the door wide enough that a really diverse group of people can get in. I may be the one who's putting in the needles, and the people in the chairs are doing the healing, but somehow the energy of the place and all the work that's gone into creating it and making it available is that manifestation.

Melody Masi

"It's truly rewarding to sit with a mom who has a great birth and can talk about it, experience it, feel it, and describe how she was totally in the present with that joy."

Melody Masi has over 40 years of experience as a Women's Health Educator. She is a psychotherapist with a Masters in Clinical Mental Health Counseling from Lesley University, and also completed her HypnoBirthing certification in 1996. Melody later designed her own program, which combines self-hypnosis, psychotherapy, and mind-body techniques to offer an individually-designed program for each birthing mom's needs. She has been helping women to birth their babies naturally on Cape Cod for over 15 years.

To find out more: mamasi@comcast.net &
www.GentleBirthingCapeCod.com & (508) 375-9899

What personal event or universal problem made you want to do what you do?

I birthed two children in a medical setting that was, in some ways, disempowering—not just for me, but for women in general. I wanted to help other women have a better experience than the one that I had. That's why I do what I do.

What has been the hardest part of doing what you do?

There are actually a number of things but the hardest part, that stands out, is convincing women of the importance of educating themselves about labor and birth before they get into the experience. Another hard piece is seeing and hearing from women who had a traumatic first birth because they didn't know the right questions to ask, or they weren't prepared to make good labor and birth choices because they didn't know. Women have the best experience when they go into labor and birth prepared, and most women don't understand that that's a key piece. When you decide you're going to have a baby, *before* you decide to get pregnant, you should research your labor and birth options. It's hard to sit with women who have been through an experience that was really disempowering or hurtful, or even traumatic, for them. They come to me because they want something different—and I know I can provide that for them—but I always feel, with great pain, the loss of that first birth experience because you never get that back.

The other part that's been hard for me is the experience of being stonewalled by medical providers who do hospital births. Medically-trained doctors aren't prepared in a way that encourages them to support natural childbirth. Many of them have never even seen a natural birth. They really don't know how to support it because they don't even know what that looks like. We need them because they're trained for problems in labor and birthing—and that's exactly when we need them—but the natural processes of pregnancy, labor, birth, and nursing have been pathologized for profit, and that encourages too many interventions that lead to non-natural births. This takes away opportunities for both moms and babies to have optimal, healthy births and that leads to problems down the road for both moms and babies. So, there are lots of things that are hard in this work. I feel like I'm swimming upstream a lot.

What keeps you going when things are tough?

When women come back to me and report how their births have gone when they're prepared—hearing the stories about how they felt empowered by their births, and feeling the joy and the love that comes both with a good labor and through those mom's words—that keeps me going. That convinces me that I'm on the right track. I know that I'm doing the right thing by listening to moms who have done this. Also, talking to other women who do this work—and knowing that I'm on the right track, hearing that they run into the same things that I do and they're inspired by the same things that I am...moms who really understand the birthing and laboring process, who are prepared and educated to make the right choices—that keeps me going. I have to really focus on those things.

What's been the most rewarding part of what you do?

The most rewarding thing is hearing moms' stories when they experience a good birth. It's amazing to witness another person's empowerment through a process that is natural and joyful. It should be easy, loving, connected, and celebratory, rather than being co-opted and taken away in a direction that doesn't let them connect with that natural process. It's truly rewarding to sit with a mom who has a great birth and can talk about it, experience it, feel it, and describe how she was totally in the present with that joy. That's truly rewarding for me.

What is the most inspiring transformation or manifestation that you've witnessed in your work?

Every natural birth story has its own inspiration but the one that comes to mind for me is a woman who came to me to be prepared for her birth. She had tried to do natural birth in two prior births and wound up in emergency C-sections. She felt that her whole birthing process had been derailed and she had a lot of trauma around that. It was really hard for her. She was pregnant again, she was an older mom, and that put her in the high-risk category (not really, but from a medical point of view, it did). She wanted, so badly, to have a VBAC (birthing vaginally after a C-section). She was willing to show up to do anything to make that happen. She went through the program, we talked it through, we did a lot of work, I connected her support from partners, and she went into the hospital in a very determined way. In fact, that's exactly what happened. It looked like she was laboring in a way that could take her down a certain road, but she knew the questions to ask and she had the right people (like her partner) to help her intervene and to keep it on the right track.

One of the greatest gifts she had was this amazing nurse, who came in and said, "We are going to do this vaginally. You are going to have this baby by natural birth. Whatever it takes, I know you can do this."

She birthed that baby naturally, vaginally, without a C-section and she avoided all medical intervention. It changed her life! She could talk freely and easily; she really got it, how that changed her life. It was healing for her to have an experience that sort of made everything right and healed the two prior experiences for her. It's always really empowering and inspirational to think of her. I think of her, because she was amazing!

Mary Raymakers

"She could completely move the right side of her body, as if she had never had a stroke. I will never forget the look on her daughter's face."

Mary Raymakers is a native of America's heartland and a graduate from the University of Wisconsin in Madison.

After exploring the corporate world, Mary discovered her true life's calling: spiritual energy healing. This calling led her to study Incan shamanism and become a full-mesa carrier from this tradition. Mary has apprenticed with Jose Luis Herrera, Isaac Millku, and Alberto Villoldo to name a few. She has also taught for Dr. Villoldo as one of his senior instructors.

After completing her apprenticeship, Mary worked with the Inca Q'ero shamans in Peru, the descendants of the original Children of the Sun rulers and healers of the Inca Empire. They are the keepers of their ancient mystery school knowledge. It was here that Mary fine-tuned her energy healing techniques for releasing deep emotional pain.

In addition to specializing in the energy medicine traditions of the Incas, Mary propelled her practice to a new level with the miraculous power of ThetaHealing™.

Mary has studied with the world's foremost relationship therapist and Good Morning America's relationship guru, Terry Real, and learned the Relational Life Therapy™ to help transform dysfunctional behavior into non-violent, full-respect living with self and others. Mary has also partnered with Terry as the Relational Life Institute's Resident Shaman Healer, and joined him at his workshops across the country for private sessions with workshop participants when their pain was activated.

Mary's private, intense sessions are unique and extraordinarily effective. Her clients range from backgrounds as diverse as medical and mental health professionals, the entertainment industry, law enforcement professionals, corporate executives, educators, housewives, children, and even pets.

To find out more: mraymakers@childrenofthesun.com & (310) 622-5704

What personal event or universal problem made you want to do what you do?

There wasn't so much a personal event or universal problem; mine was kind of a journey. I was working for a company, and a friend of mine would periodically invite me to attend fun events with her. I've had a strong spiritual base since 1994 and these events were always spiritually based. So, one night she asked me to attend this lecture-workshop on soul retrieval. I had heard of it before, I'd even been in one and felt nothing, and I wanted to see if this could be a different experience with somebody different.

Even though I went there with my friend, the person who ended up being my first teacher said to us, "Find a total stranger and give your first name only. I'm going to walk you through how to do a little bit of soul retrieval. When I bring you back out of the maze of it, you'll share with each other and then we'll share as a group."

So, this woman was a total stranger—she had given me her first name only—and she was telling me things that a lot of my family and friends didn't even know about me.

My mouth dropped like, "This is absolutely unbelievable!"

Then, when I shared with her what I had found for her, she said the same thing.

There were 25 to 30 people in the group, and when we shared as a group, *they* all said the same thing, "Oh, my gosh! I can't believe they were telling me things that they couldn't possibly know!"

At the end of the group, the teacher announced, "I teach this and more."

I thought: *Wow, this man really has something here. I'd like to get trained in what he's doing.*

In my first training session with him, I knew, immediately, that this was what I was on the planet to do, that this was my purpose for being here. Before I had found this, people would always say, "Do what you love and you'll get paid for it." And I used to say to people, "The only thing I'm really good at is loving people, and people aren't going to pay me to do that." So, finding that first teacher, in the work I do as a shaman, actually was the catalyst for putting me into doing what I do today.

What has been the hardest part of doing what you do?

Because my work is so transformative with people and I see them going back to ways they were created and designed to be, the hardest part is feeling like: *how do I get the word out on a mass scale?* I have trained others, so people don't have to see *me*, per se, but I really want the world to know, "You no longer have to live in pain. You no longer have to suffer."

This is the analogy I use now: I feel like I'm a doctor and I'm in the middle of a plague. The antidote for the plague is in my little black doctor bag. Nobody knows that I'm the doctor with the little black doctor bag, and everyone's dying around me or very sick with the plague. How do I let people know that I've got their antidote to get rid of the plague, to get rid of whatever it is they're suffering from? That has probably been the hardest part of my job. It's an ancient technique but it's very newly reintroduced to the world, so it seems as if it's brand new. I wonder: *How do I get something out to the world that's so new and effective, in a way that people know they can, first off, get out of pain and suffering, and secondly, find someone like me to help them get out of it?*

What keeps you going when things are tough?

I would probably use the same analogy: I know I have what people need. I know the different healing modalities that my clients and I have experienced and as good as many of them are, none come close to the powerful, complete release of this shamanic healing modality. I've done this work for twelve and a half years and everyone says to me, "Oh, my gosh! Do you know how much money I could have saved if I had known about you when I was a kid?" or, "Do you know that, in two hours, you just released what I've tried to get rid of my entire life?" I *know*, deep in my core—every cell in my body knows—that what I have is what the world needs right now. So, when I think about how I'm not seeing as many people as I'd like to, I *know* this is what I'm here to do and I just pour all my energy into having people find me. That's really what keeps me going. It's really that same analogy: I've got the antidote. I just have to find the people who have the plague.

What's been the most rewarding part of what you do?

The most rewarding part, for me, is that the lives of every single person I work with are changed for the better. My work is about getting rid of people's emotional pain. When, at the end of their session, their eyes are shining, and they look—and feel—like when they were a kid, the most rewarding part is them looking like the way they were created and designed to be. I know that I played a part in getting them there, so every single person is an inspiration to me because I know that they're free. It's difficult to put it into words. To know that people's lives have returned to being joyful, happy, and they now have more energy to put into making their dreams come true, they will now make a difference in the world because they're no longer carrying their pain. When other people look at them and say, "What's different? I want what you've got!" they can reply,

"It's because I'm not in pain. I can tell you how to get there." It's like a ripple effect going out and I know that I'm playing my part in changing the world. Right now, in my tradition, there are prophecies just like the Mayans' that say this is the time of great transition. We're *really* going to start evolving into the people we were designed to be, the way Spirit, or Source, (or whatever you want to call it) designed and created us to be. On a planetary scale, we're going to get there. So, with every single person I work, we're that much closer to it happening. There is nothing more rewarding than watching somebody be free from pain.

What is the most inspiring transformation or manifestation that you've witnessed in your work?

I've had many miracles happen but, I'd say, my first miracle was the biggie. I had been doing this for about four years, I was living in Hawaii, and, for the first time, I had fliers made.

A woman called me right before the holidays. She didn't know about me (except for having seen my flier) but she said, "I would like to give a session with you to every member of my family. If I pay you to work on my entire family, will you come to my home?"

It wasn't a huge family, there were six people I would be working with, and I said, "Absolutely! I'll go anywhere to help anyone."

The woman who had called lived on the other side of the island. When I got there, the first one I worked on was her mother-in-law who was 84. Her husband had passed away six months earlier and she'd had a stroke when she was 79, which left the right side of her body almost completely paralyzed. They didn't tell me until later, but the family hoped she would get some peace of mind after losing her husband. So, I just did what I do—I started working on her to release her emotional pain—and all of a sudden, her right side started to spasm. I didn't think anything of it because I was so locked into being focused on helping her release her emotional pain. Her daughter (not the one who had hired me, but one who was there from the Los Angeles area) was sitting in the room because, she had said, "My mother forgets things and I would like to tell my mom what had happened, in case she asks me."

I heard the daughter say, "Oh, my goodness!"

All I did was focus on the mother and all I said was, "Breathe through it," because that's part of what I do, and all of a sudden, her paralysis was completely *gone!*

When we were done, she sat up and when she could stand up and move, the daughter was crying. She was in shock, and I was in shock, thinking: *Oh, my goodness, my work really does work!* And she was paralysis-free! She could completely move the right side of her body, as if she had never had a stroke. I will never forget the look on her daughter's face. Again, I don't have words to describe how I felt inside when I realized that my working with her—not expecting to free her paralysis, but just to get her out of her emotional pain—completely got rid of that paralysis. That was the biggest thing that stuck with me.

Arts & Education

Aziza Browne

"Whenever there's a huge breakdown, I know that some huge difference or change in my life is right around the corner."

Aziza Browne is a glass artist and jewelry designer. As a classically trained artist with a BFA in Visual Art, she created her jewelry line, Aziza Jewelry, in 2003 and has been making jewelry and teaching glass bead making for several years. Aziza Jewelry combines glass beads, natural gemstones, sterling silver, and solid gold into gorgeous one-of-a-kind customizable pieces for everyday wear, as well as for a variety of special occasions.

Aziza has taught glass bead making at leading industry glass studios such as Urban Glass and Tecnolux in Brooklyn, New York. Her jewelry can be purchased online at www.AzizaJewelry.com.

To find out more: www.AzizaJewelry.com & aziza@azizajewelry.com

What personal event or universal problem made you want to do what you do?

I never consciously made the decision to become a jewelry designer. I thought I would be a ceramic artist after college, and that one day I would own my own ceramic art gallery, featuring my work and other artists' ceramic work. But while I was in college, I became very interested in glass. One of my friends took a class and she was telling me how awesome it was. Since there were no glass courses offered in my college, I found one after I graduated. It turned out that it was a glass bead-making class, and I was already interested in jewelry design (I started making jewelry when I was about eight or nine) so it was perfect. I took the class, and working on a hot gas torch, manipulating the hot glass, and working with these shaping tools came so naturally to me. I was also encouraged because my teachers were so impressed at how good I was when they realized this was my first time working with glass.

At first, I just made glass beads and jewelry for myself. I wore it every day, everywhere I went, and soon people started noticing my unique handmade jewelry and commenting on how great they thought it was. Strangers, on the subway even, would approach me and ask me about it. Everyone seemed to want my jewelry. From pretty early on, my coworkers were commenting on how great they thought my jewelry was, and they just knew I was going to be selling my own jewelry, full-time, and making a real career out of it. Looking back, I think it's amazing that some of these people foresaw that happening from the very beginning, and that they had such faith in me.

The support was really incredible, even from the beginning. My jewelry became pretty popular in my small circle of friends and family. Everyone was asking me to make customized jewelry. At first, I was just making it for the women—friends, coworkers, and family. Then my dad, brother, and a couple of male friends started requesting some custom-made pieces, which I thought was pretty funny. Being my own model and wearing my own jewelry has really paid off for me; that's how I got started in the jewelry design business.

What has been the hardest part of doing what you do?

There are two different aspects. From a business point of view, the hardest part is trying to foresee which pieces I create will actually sell or not and trying to predict their future popularity. It's difficult because I fund my own business with my profits, so I purchase all the materials using my own money. If something doesn't sell, I'm stuck with it. I also create unique, one-of-a-kind, and customizable pieces, but at the same time I try to be both on trend with the seasons and what's going in on the world, and make pieces that are timeless, fun, and wearable for everyday occasions. So, it's been hard to predict what's going to sell, be creative, and not have a bunch of stock left over.

The other hard part—because I make all of my own jewelry—is balancing my work life and my personal life. That's really hard, but I do the best I can.

What keeps you going when things are tough?

I keep all of my customer email praises in a folder. When things are tough and I'm having a bad day, or I'm feeling really stuck, or I don't think I can push through, I look over those emails. I love to read how a customer's wife loved the necklace that I made for her with their new baby's name on it, or how someone's daughter hasn't taken the piece off all week long, or how I helped to make their occasion really special, or something like that. Those praise emails really keep me going when things are tough.

I also have a small group of artist friends and other entrepreneurs who all support each other. I think it's really important, when you're an entrepreneur, to have a small group—or any group—of friends or other entrepreneurs who think like you and face similar challenges, so that you can all support each other.

At the end of the day, I'm a really driven person and I know that I have a bigger purpose in life. Even when times get tough, I have this inner knowing that whenever I have a huge breakdown, a breakthrough is right around the corner. I know that might sound cheesy, but it's usually that exact scenario that happens for me every time. Whenever there's a huge breakdown, I know that some huge difference or change in my life is right around the corner.

What's been the most rewarding part of what you do?

As a jewelry designer and businesswoman, just by doing what I do, I get to be happy! I get to be creative every day and inspire other people to live their dreams. That was never my goal, but it's a nice result. I really believe that we should be doing what makes us happy for our careers. It's rewarding to inspire someone else to live their dreams and do what they love, instead of what they feel they *have* to do as a career. I really think that work should be enjoyable and easy, or at least enjoyable. It saddens me that so many people are miserable working jobs they can't stand—or maybe it's not that they can't stand it but they just don't enjoy it—in order to pay bills and support themselves and their families, thinking that they have no other choice.

What is the most inspiring transformation or manifestation that you've witnessed in your work?

The most inspiring transformation I've witnessed within my work has been within myself. I never saw myself as an influential person or as a businesswoman until this past year. Being in business for myself has created these aspects of who I am. It's forced me to grow myself, getting myself out there and meeting new people and growing my business. It has required me to make a huge shift, at times, to thinking of myself as a creative person and artist, but also as a businesswoman who is in business to make a living and a profit by sharing my gifts and my talents, which is my jewelry. It's fun to do what I do because I get to be creative and design new pieces all the time. It's not always fun to think about keeping daily routines, marketing, keeping track of details like website statistics, how to drive more traffic, and so on. I'm a driven person, but keeping a disciplined routine never came naturally to me; in fact, it's still a challenge. Even though the behind-the-scenes work is sometimes more challenging than fun, it's necessary for me to know what's going on. Keeping track of technical things, like ordering supplies and accounting, hasn't been fun, but it's required me to transform my thinking and be well rounded in that way.

Zoë Vincent

"To transform other people's lives through my experiences, my joy, and my love of children is probably the greatest gift of all!"

Zoë Vincent is the owner of Giggles n' Gifts. She started the company in honor of her two amazing granddaughters who inspire her beyond words. Her online store carries quality gifts and products without a huge price tag. You'll find things that are colorful and some are just plain silly. Zoë describes her online store as, "A ton of fun with a splash of practical." It's a one stop shopping experience and all gifts are between $10 and $30.

As well as being an online business owner, Zoë is a member of The Agape International Choir in Culver City, California. The choir is 250 singers strong, performing at The Agape International Spiritual Center and touring the country raising their voices for sold out venues and churches.

To find out more: www.GigglesNGifts.com & gigglesngifts@yahoo.com & (818) 912-9591

What personal event or universal problem made you want to do what you do?

I was in an auto accident almost two years ago. I had a near-death experience and I was spoken to by angels. They told me several projects that I was to do; one is happening right now and two are in the works.

What has been the hardest part of doing what you do?

One project is a book and the angels gave me the name of it. I'm not exactly sure I have an idea of what it's supposed to be about. So, I'm waiting for some new downloads.

The one I'm actually doing is a children's store called Giggles n' Gifts. The hardest part is keeping the faith and knowing that the customers will come.

What keeps you going when things are tough?

What keeps me going is knowing that the children's store brings so much joy to others. It's funny, when my grandchildren come over and the door to my office is shut (because that's where all the toys are), they knock on the door and say, "Grandma?" I know that there are tons of other kids who would be thrilled to have what I have; it will bring smiles to so many children's faces.

What's been the most rewarding part of what you do?

The most rewarding part is smiles! Smiles on little ones' faces and people getting excited to find unique things to give to their babies, their grandchildren, the children in their lives…that's super rewarding.

What is the most inspiring transformation or manifestation that you've witnessed in your work?

I'm not sure that I have actually hit that point yet but I think it is me being here to carry out, and to be able to complete, what the angels told me in the car accident, as opposed to what the other possibility could have been (that I might not to be here). To transform other people's lives through my experiences, my joy, and my love of children is probably the greatest gift of all!

Gaill Blackburn

"I'm at a point in my life where it's not about me and it's not about anything else; it's about letting go of ego and letting God work through me."

Passionate about helping others to live their absolute best life possible, Gaill Blackburn is a wife and mother as well as author, healer, speaker, and non-profit co-founder. She considers herself a rather eclectic entrepreneur, with a BS in Business Management, an AA in Construction Drafting, and a diverse background consisting of art, graphics, construction, business, project management, computers, web design, writing, and various forms of energy healing. Her lofty career ambitions took a drastic turn when she gave birth to a beautiful, differently-abled daughter in 1997 and realized what was truly important in life. She left corporate America to care for her daughter and subsequently immersed herself in the world of Volunteerism.

Gaill is happily married to Bret, a two-time traumatic brain injury survivor, and mom to Britney, who has already endured over 20 surgeries. Her family is her life, and she revels in her husband and daughter's determination to not let anything get them down. She is the Co-Founder of Motivational Small Talk Inc., a non-profit corporation that specializes in bully prevention, diversity and dwarfism awareness, disability education, and motivational speaking. Gaill started asking God to use her as a vessel to share His love and a vehicle to spread his word over a decade ago and has been led on a spiritual quest ever since. She has studied a variety of healing methods, and as most healers, developed her own style encompassing parts of each of them.

Gaill absolutely loves helping others, and feels incredibly blessed to achieve this through her God given gifts for which she is eternally grateful.

To find out more: www. GaillBlackburn.com & www.MotivationalSmallTalk.org & www.AngelicHealingsLLC.com

What personal event or universal problem made you want to do what you do?

I don't know if I can narrow it down to just one; it's the way my life has unfolded altogether. When I got married, my husband was a little quirky. It didn't bother me when I found out that he actually had a brain injury, and I didn't understand all the ramifications of that at the time. Anyway, we got married. We're still married and have a great relationship. We went through everything—infertility treatments, a high risk pregnancy, the loss of a twin, and an emergency C-section. Our daughter was born with her own set of challenges. She's "differently-abled," I like to say, instead of disabled, because she definitely shows people that she can do everything her own way. She was born with a form of dwarfism called achondroplasia, and she also has hydrocephalus, which is fluid on the brain. Now she's 15, has endured well over 20 surgeries, and is definitely the strongest person I have ever met.

During all of my daughter's challenges, my husband and I had our own handyman business and were doing very well, when he took a nose-dive off a two-story roof, putting up Christmas lights for a client, and he sustained his second brain injury. I can't explain it, but after I got over the initial shock and our family found our new "normal," I thought: *How many families have multiple disabilities in them—not just one brain injury, but two, and not just one surgery, but over twenty?* It was as if God was trying to hit me over the head with a two-by-four and I hadn't been listening. All of a sudden, I started to realize that there was so much more to life. I had been going through the motions. So, I started this spiritual quest, and it's led me into the most incredible life changes. I used to be about, "Money, money, money…got to make money!" Then, after my daughter was born, I immersed myself in the world of volunteerism to help other parents discover the very special gifts in their own differently-abled children. Now, I've taken it a step further, I've gotten into energy healing, and I've realized how everything is energy and how we can raise our vibrations to hold more love, light, and peace and make our own Heaven on Earth here. I've immersed myself in learning different modalities of healing and I, like most people do, have put it together in my own way.

I'm at a point in my life where it's not about me and it's not about anything else; it's about letting go of ego and letting God work through me. Wonderful miracles have happened by just being in that place of grace, where you *can* put your ego aside and let God just work through you. It's not me healing people by any means, it's God! To be able to do that has been phenomenal. It's not just healing others, it's healing myself as well.

What has been the hardest part of doing what you do?

I think the hardest part is realizing how many people out there so identify with their pain or their dis-ease that they are unwilling to give it up, or they're so status quo with literally living in their own Hell on Earth that they can't fathom that life could be different. I have such empathy for people, and I desperately want to help people to live the best life possible. I have to stand back and realize they're on their own path and they have to take their own direction. It's not about me. Even if I know I can help them, it's about knowing I can't push it and they're going to stay that way. It hurts, but it's just part of it.

What keeps you going when things are tough?

What keeps me going is my faith. I truly believe that everything happens for a reason.

Some people look at my life and say, "Oh, my God, you've been through so much! I don't know how you can handle it!"

I just look at everything that's happened to me, and to my family, as gifts because I don't take for granted what a lot of people do. I know when you have a child who's had so many serious surgeries, you really appreciate each day to its fullest. My husband, with two brain injuries, and my daughter, with all her challenges…they never give up. They give me so much strength. Anybody who's considered disabled and doesn't let that label define who they are, and rises up to any challenge, they're my heroes. That really keeps me going, to see other people trying their hardest not just to strive through life, but to thrive through it and be the best they can be. My daughter could have just sat down and not tried a lot of things, but she's thriving in high school. She's a sophomore now, and starting in her freshman year she was the basketball manager of all three girls' basketball teams! She proudly wears the number "1/2" on her jersey, and gives 200 percent to the team. She's doing everything she can, and it's so empowering to see somebody with that much ambition and stick-to-itiveness, who doesn't know the meaning of the word "no." She's not going to let anybody stop her, and that keeps me going more than anything.

What's been the most rewarding part of what you do?

Being able to change lives and help people realize that, energetically, everything's a choice. I don't really feel that there are true victims out there; I feel we all make choices that either let light, love, and joy into our lives, or let fear, depression, and things like that in. To help people make that shift to realize that they are in control of their lives and they don't have to passively accept everything that happens to them, that they can actually design their own lives and live the best lives possible—and to see the looks on their faces when they get it, and to hear back later about how different their lives are—to me, those are the biggest rewards in the world.

What is the most inspiring transformation or manifestation that you've witnessed in your work?

That would be my mom healing herself of cancer. She's 81 years old, and she's another one of my heroes. She was diagnosed with breast cancer and, of course, the surgeon said immediately that she had to have it cut out. I feel my path to energy work has been God-led every step of the way. For an 81-year-old to be open to energetic work for the first time in her life is a miracle! She has really embraced being healed through energy. I'm not saying I'm the one healing her; she's received multiple healings with different modalities, and it is all God's work.

One of the most profound spiritual experiences I've ever had in my life was at a healing ceremony—a fire ceremony where we do healings. My mom doesn't understand a lot of what I do, but she accepts it. She'll say things like, "It's way above my head. I don't understand all this, but I see the change in you and I see how you're helping people, and that's all that counts."

After this particular fire ceremony, which was after her diagnosis, I was sitting there meditating and this dark shadow came up to my right side. At first, I was kind of taken aback and a little apprehensive.

I asked, "Are you of true Christ consciousness?"

It answered, "Yes."

Then I realized, after I let go and got my ego out of the way, that it was my mom's spirit, and she had come to the healing fire.

When it came to the part where they asked if there were any spirits in the land who wanted a healing, I said, "Mom, go!"

She replied, "No, not yet."

I didn't understand what she was saying.

"This is your chance!"

"No, be patient."

I just stepped back and then the leader did something different that he's never done at any of the ceremonies I'd been to.

He said, "If there are any spirits still in-body who have come to this fire for a healing, come to the fire now."

And my mom went to it.

Even though my mom doesn't understand how all this works, to know that at 81 years old, her spirit is so strong to live and to want to make everything she can out of life, and to have her there, 60 miles away from her house, was the most incredible experience I've ever had.

I told the leader afterward, "Wow, my mom was here!"

And he said, "I know! Who do you think told me? That's why I did it differently."

To have the acknowledgement that even the leader knew she was there was phenomenal. If you can just get to a point where you can let go of thinking something's impossible, and just be at that point of grace, faith, and belief that the impossible can be possible, there are so many miracles in the world that happen all the time. That was probably the biggest miracle that I've ever, ever witnessed. It was phenomenal. My wish for the world would be that everyone could experience such grace in their lifetime.

Kelly Corsino

*"No matter how many gadgets we invent, or how many cultures
come and go, shift and change, one thing that seems present,
everywhere in the human experience, is music."*

Kelly Corsino's music, talks, and workshops are a celebration of awakening. Her work is a masterful combination of deep spiritual messages that touch the heart and lift the soul. As a gifted vocalist, Kelly has the versatility to sing like a pure, sweet angel or to powerfully belt out a tune to rock your core, with mastery akin to Aretha Franklin. Kelly has been honored with two LA Music Awards—one for Best Female Vocalist and another for Best New Artist—as well as three Posi Music Award nominations.

It was at age seven that Kelly began her career as a professional musician, when she joined the family band. Eventually, she was led to film and TV; however, it has always been her music that has guided her along the way. She is a tour de force of innovating music styles.

As a student of life, Kelly has studied the Spiritual Wisdom of the ages from shamans and Buddhist priests, and the scriptures and sutras of masters such as Jesus the Christ, Meister Eckhart, and Ernest Holmes.

Kelly brings ancient teachings and her own personal experiences into her inspirational singing, speaking, and workshops, empowering others to reach their highest potential and joy!

To find out more: www.KellyCorsino.com & kelly@kellycorsino.com & (714) 827-0889

What personal event or universal problem made you want to do what you do?

I believe that the world is hungry for more positive messages and music delivered in a really powerful way. Music has the ability to transport us in time, space, and emotional state. Have you ever noticed that you can be in a really bummed-out mood and, suddenly, a really fun song comes on and you're instantly transported? It is compelling and encouraging to know that something as primal as music, that has been a part of the human experience since the dawn of civilized humans, still has that kind of power. No matter how many gadgets we invent, or how many cultures come and go, shift and change, one thing that seems present, everywhere in the human experience, is music. I see a paradigm shift happening and there are a lot of folks, all over the planet, craving harmony, balance, and joy. I love that I'm being called to make music that speaks to that. The inspirational speaking I've been doing has been a wonderful way to go even deeper with the teachings, once the heart and mind have been opened with music.

What has been the hardest part of doing what you do?

The hardest part has been the amount of faith required of me to keep jumping without a net. When I first started on this path, whenever I was called to say yes to an opportunity, the businesswoman in me would worry: *How the heck is this gonna work out?* I have always earned a really great living as a musician, so learning to look at a gig from any perspective, other than the bottom line, was difficult. Learning to *really* listen to that still, small voice to figure out what to say "yes" to was the most challenging thing of all. That process, alone, caused me to grow tremendously on this path. All of my old stories kept coming up, so I was forced to keep addressing them over and over. Oftentimes, the scenarios differed greatly from one to the next, so I really did feel as though I was starting from scratch with regard to saying "yes" or "no" to a question of whether or not to record a particular song, write with a co-writer, or take a performance opportunity.

I still find myself coming up against my "stuff." I think God has a great sense of humor!

What keeps you going when things are tough?

What keeps me going is prayer, prayer, prayer! It's funny, I used to think that prayer was very formal and sometimes, for me, it still is; however, more often than not, my prayer process around tough moments involves setting the question into motion, directing it to God (or Spirit or my Higher Self—or whatever I feel like calling It in that moment), and then remembering to leave some quiet time to *listen*. I think the most important thing for me to learn how to do, when things are tough, is to listen. I've learned that listening is a full sensory experience: What is showing up in my world? Are there butterflies or dung beetles? What are people saying? Is there a theme to what I keep hearing, seeing, and smelling? I am learning how to use my whole body to listen. I also find it really important to reach out to people whom I respect to help remind me of my Truth and lift me up. God uses people!

What's been the most rewarding part of what you do?

The most rewarding part has been having someone tell me that they felt a peace inside, after hearing one of my songs or talks, because they had been struggling with something very similar to what inspired the talk or the song; they felt relief, knowing they were not alone. This connection of souls, and the feeling that I can actually make a difference just by sharing my process, is hugely rewarding.

It's also really satisfying when people tell me that my music brings them joy. I've had folks tell me they love to pop my disc in when they're stuck in traffic because it makes them happy. I laughed so hard when a gal told me she was rocking out to my disc with the windows down, and had another driver ask her who was on the radio because she wanted to tune in the station.

What is the most inspiring transformation or manifestation that you've witnessed in your work?

In addition to so many beautiful and amazing moments with people who have shared their stories with me when I'm on the road, I'd have to say the biggest transformation has been in me. I used to suffer greatly from depression, and I had a lot of old stories that weighed me down and kept me from taking flight. I have been on a self-aware spiritual journey since my mid-twenties, but when I got the call to start taking what I had learned and bringing it to others through my music and my talks, I was given the opportunity to go deeper with the work than I had ever gone before. I guess you could say that I realized I needed to save myself before I could ever hope to save the world.

Erik Peterson

*"Working with people who are very talented, very in touch
with the God within, that is the most joyous thing...
just to know I'm on the same page with someone,
spiritually as well as musically."*

Erik Peterson's innate ability to communicate his music through an open heart is apparent to anyone who hears him sing. Healing others with his music is what inspires him to write and perform, and to compose inspirational music for artists all over the world.

Although music had always come naturally to Erik, he decided to further his musical knowledge by obtaining a degree from the Berklee College of Music in Boston. It was there that Erik received the experience and the tools necessary to become a professional recording artist, giving him the confidence needed to produce five CDs entitled, *Piano Meditations, Always the Season, This Time Around,* and *We Are Here.* His latest CD, *ALIVE,* explores the courage and beauty of being a survivor by overcoming personal heartbreak and loss, and moving to a space of inner strength.

In addition to writing and producing records, Erik has also provided uplifting live music for many well-known authors, including Neale Donald Walsch, Marianne Williamson, Deepak Chopra, Mark Victor Hansen, Della Reese, Les Brown, Rev. Michael Beckwith, and Famous Amos, to name a few.

In addition to his solo performances, Erik has shared the stage with many other well-known artists, such as Grammy winners Paula Cole, Jonny Lang, and Taj Mahal, Warren Hill, Carly Simon, Earth Wind and Fire's Al McKay, and jazz great Barbara Morrison.

Erik continues to uplift and inspire thousands of people in all parts of the world. His life is about music, his music is about love, and his message is about inspiration.

To find out more: (860) 933-8691 & studiofourty@att.net

What personal event or universal problem made you want to do what you do?

It's a lot deeper than that for me. I've known that I was going to do this since I was four or five years old. What keeps me doing it is seeing people in the world who need to feel love and connection with a Higher Power. That keeps me doing it. It also keeps me doing it because it's my own therapy, in a way; it really gets me in touch with myself and makes me a more well-rounded person. I do that for other people as well. It's a beautiful thing.

What has been the hardest part of doing what you do?

The hardest part is when I know there are people who are just *not* receptive to what I have to say. I know it's the truth, I know I'm singing about love, I know I'm singing about peace, and people are just blocked to that. But my faith says that the more I do it, the more I spread my joy around and help others find their joy, the more other people will discover theirs as well. I'd say that's the hardest thing, when I see people resisting the truth of who they are.

What keeps you going when things are tough?

What keeps me going is the faith that it is all good in the Universe, and that things circulate. For example, when it comes to tithing—when it comes to giving and receiving—to keep that circle going is so important and so vital. A lot of people hold on and they save, and they don't give from the abundant flow because they're stuck. So, when I'm in those times when I'm feeling stuck and I'm having a hard time keeping going,

I try to tune in to that energy of the circulation; I give. In fact, I'm doing a couple of projects right now for which I'm not even charging the people because I really believe in what they're doing, and it comes back! It comes back to me. But you don't do it with the intent of: *I'm doing this so I can get something back.* You do it from the abundance of your own heart and the abundance of your soul, and it just comes back to you in such a beautiful way.

What's been the most rewarding part of what you do?

Working with people who are very talented, very in touch with the God within, that is the most joyous thing…just to know I'm on the same page with someone, spiritually as well as musically. Recently, I wrote, produced, and recorded some songs with Keith Leon; we wrote five songs in four days. This session was a manifestation of what it's like when things just flow with ease and grace. When all the factors are there, it's such a pleasure and I get such joy from that! When you get that lyric right or when you get that one melody right, it just feels so good inside. It just moves you, you know? That's the thing, for sure.

What is the most inspiring transformation or manifestation that you've witnessed in your work?

A good friend of mine, J. Karen Thomas, when she first moved to Los Angeles, was doing a little acting but she was very insecure about her singing, so she wasn't singing. I asked her to be in this show, a benefit fundraiser I was doing, and she was so humble and grateful.

"I can't believe you're having me sing in this!"

Now I'm just looking at where she has come to since then, and thinking I had a part in that that I gave her her first singing job, or singing opportunity, and made her look at herself and say: *I am a singer! I am really great at what I do! I have an amazing voice!*

She went on to do all these wonderful things, and she continues to do wonderful things. That was definitely a very, very rewarding story for me.

There's one more story I'd like to tell you about. I played at a church—I think it was Joan Steadman's church—up in Northern California.

This lady came up to me and said, "Erik, I just want you to know that the last time you were here, I bought your CD. I was planning on killing myself the next day, and when I listened to your music, I changed my mind."

That just blew me the heck away!

I was like, "Oh, my God, can I give you the biggest hug right now?"

She said, "Absolutely."

When you play the small church or the small venue, you don't think people are listening because there are only a few people in the audience. But it's just as important as playing an amphitheatre, because you're changing that one life. You're changing the trajectory of that one soul, and that's powerful.

Nioshi Jackson

*"The most rewarding part is helping people make their dreams come true...
helping people have their "aha" moments...helping people demystify
the process to create music and pursue a career."*

Nioshi Jackson is a go-to live/tour and session musician in Music City. He has worked with the likes of Trisha Yearwood, Michael McDonald, Larry Carlton, Ricky Skaggs, BB King's Soul Brigade, Chester Thompson, Bobby Keys, Crystal Taliefero, Victor Wooten, and a laundry list of others. Having played all over the country (in 49 states, to be exact) and having had his passport stamped in over 10 countries, Nioshi is now focused on what's next in his career growth. He formed his own band, The Nioshi Jackson Reason, released the CD of the same name in early 2011, and has since launched The Explosion Group.

Already an accomplished musical director and producer, Nioshi is setting out to utilize the wisdom of his Music Management mentor, Doc McGhee, to provide artist management services, music production, and consultation. The goal is to help aspiring musicians *explode* into the reality of being successful, knowledgeable working musicians.

Having worked in practically every major genre of music, Nioshi is well-suited to the task. He understands that opportunity, matched with preparation, is the equivalent of potential energy. "I have a well-rounded history in the business. I've been mentored by some of the best in the industry," says Nioshi. He knows, from experience, that an artist must achieve and maintain the delicate balance of creative force meeting business acumen. Most importantly, he understands that honesty, in the creative process, is requisite to success. If Nioshi Jackson's career, thus far, is *any* indication, his neighbors on Music Row had better "brace for impact."

To find out more: n@theexplosiongroup.com & (615) 601-1904

What personal event or universal problem made you want to do what you do?

Ultimately, the music business, by itself, is pretty scary. If you're not aware of how it works or if you don't know anyone who can show you, it can seem impossible to get into. I'm fortunate enough to have been in the business virtually my whole life, so I've studied it and been fascinated with it from a very young age. The older I got and the more success I had as a drummer, I thought: *How can I help others, beyond just playing the drums or just holding a beat for somebody?* I saw artists with so much promise all of a sudden just disappear, and I wasn't sure why. I came to find out that it usually had something to do with bad management or bad counsel; they trusted the wrong people, who basically led their careers to ruin. After going back and forth, I believed I could really guide people's careers if I knew enough to start reaching out on that level. To reach out, I launched The Explosion Group, a management firm and production facility, where I also do my consultations. The consultations are what I am most passionate about because I'm actually one-on-one with artists, helping them find their way—not just in the marketplace but discovering what their true voice or true calling is, from a musical standpoint.

What has been the hardest part of doing what you do?

Other than the typical new business struggles—financial or whatever else—I think that the most difficult part is helping people de-program all the negativity they've grown to accept over the years. So many people have dreams when they're younger, then life happens, they put that dream on a shelf, and then it gets dusty. When something else gets put in front of them, the next thing you know, they've forgotten their dream is even on the shelf. So, when they finally get to that point when they realize that life is too short and they really want to do something, they'll reach out—but when I show them how easy it really is, it kind of freaks them out. They start going back into those negative beliefs of, "I can't do that. I could never do that." Nothing could be farther from the truth, but they've accepted it for so long that it takes a while to chip away at it.

I read, once, that for every time somebody tells you that you can't do something, it takes sixteen times of somebody telling you that you *can* to eradicate that *one*. If you've had a bunch of people who have thought that maybe you're crazy for getting into the music business—or that you don't have a gift with your voice, or your instrument, or whatever else—and you've heard that enough times growing up, you start to believe it. So, when one person says, "No, you really can!"—in your mind, it's not enough. The most difficult part, for me, is helping clients break through the negativity and getting them to really see the potential that does exist within them.

What keeps you going when things are tough?

What keeps me going is prayer! I'm learning more about meditation. I'm an avid reader; I read all the time. I'm always learning. I listen to a lot of Keith Jarrett's solo piano, when it gets tough for me. I put that on, light some candles, and de-stress.

What's been the most rewarding part of what you do?

The most rewarding part is helping people make their dreams come true...helping people have their "aha" moments...helping people demystify the process to create music and pursue a career. Not everybody wants to go out and be a mega-star; some people just want to have a piece of music they can call their own. Helping them get that provides so much pride for them and gives them a sense of accomplishment. It makes them really feel good about themselves, and they believe they actually can do it, because they now have a product—a CD in their hands, an mp3 they can listen to on their computer—something they can give to their friends and family, or sell, and they start having shows. From there, it spirals into whatever they want it to be. Helping people get to that place, knowing I had a part in that, is the most rewarding thing. Helping others get where they want to go, in a way that there's no pressure and that's easy to understand, is why I do this. It's very fulfilling for me to be a part of that journey.

What is the most inspiring transformation or manifestation that you've witnessed in your work?

I'd have to say that the most inspiring transformation has been in my own life. My whole life, I thought I would be a drummer. Not that being a drummer is bad—I enjoy it very much—but I never knew that I would have enough experience and wisdom to help others in this capacity. Now that I'm aware of what's been placed in me, the responsibility—the call, if you will—keeps me going. It keeps me learning and I'm inspired by the changes that come through me so I'm able to help my clients. The more I learn, the more I can help them. Helping more than one person at a time is a beautiful thing, and I'm truly grateful for this new life.

Cathi Stevenson

"I'm really fortunate in doing what I do because it rarely seems like work. In fact, most days I can't believe people pay me to do this."

Becoming a book cover designer was a natural progression for Cathi Stevenson, who has a degree in Psychology and English, and a strong background in printing and publishing that goes back to 1981. She also worked as a writer, editor, and page designer for the advertising department of the largest newspaper in Atlantic Canada.

Having worked alongside the presses, Cathi can offer sound advice based on practical experience when it comes to designing for print, and her advertising background means she pays special attention to how your book cover will look online. That small thumbnail is one of the most important promotional tools your book has; that is why her company, Book Cover Express, specializes in creating clean designs that are eye-catching both online and off.

To find out more: www.BookCoverExpress.com

What personal event or universal problem made you want to do what you do?

I don't think there was any one event. Publishing just seemed like an industry I was always destined to work in, even from a young age. I've worked as both a writer and a designer. A few years ago, I reconnected with an uncle I had not seen in many years. When I told him what I do, he said he wasn't surprised. He told me that when I was very young and stayed with him and his wife, I would spend hours cutting up magazines and rearranging the page layouts.

What has been the hardest part of doing what you do?

One of the challenges I've faced is being asked to design a cover, and I'm sure it's not the right design for the book. There's not much you can do in this case, other than share your ideas. People have reasons for wanting what they want, but if the client insists on the design, I usually try to create at least one of the proofs with an alternative cover that I think is the better way to go. Sometimes it works; sometimes it doesn't. The important thing is the client is happy.

What keeps you going when things are tough?

Mostly the mortgage payment is what keeps me going (joking). I'm really fortunate in doing what I do because it rarely seems like work. In fact, most days I can't believe people pay me to do this. Most of my income comes from cover design, but when I do need a break, I accept writing assignments or temporary day jobs. I always miss designing after a while, though and I'm lucky to be able to work on book covers in the evenings and on weekends to relax. I never stray far.

What's been the most rewarding part of what you do?

The most rewarding part, quite simply, is being able to create something. I also like being able to work from home, work my own hours, and choose my own clients.

What is the most inspiring transformation or manifestation that you've witnessed in your work?

Many years ago, I found a great mentor who was not shy about telling me what I needed to fix and improve upon. Every harsh word from her was gold to me. She was an awesome designer, but has since retired from the industry. She had a great impact on the way I design book covers.

Marlene Harper

"The key is that you can live your life to the fullest—that you can be you,
be yourself, be who you're meant to be, be empowered—
and create the life that you want to create."

Marlene Grace Harper is an actress, a puppeteer, and a mother of four beautiful children. She has spent a lifetime working in different levels of theater, including writing and directing productions. Locally, she's acted in over 20 shows at the Heritage Theatre. She performed puppetry with Susan Neidert at Fine Arts Center. She's a core actress in the Martin Harris Pageant and, internationally, she has performed and toured in British Columbia, Canada.

Marlene has a B.F.A. Degree with a major in Theatre and a minor in Communication, from Utah State University (USU), a Master of Arts in Education degree, from George Wythe University (GWU), and is currently working on a Doctorate in Education and Constitutional Law at GWU.

Her work with youth, local community, and in the arts has been met with much recognition and appreciation. Marlene has received many awards including Woman of the Year (American Biographical Institute), an International Peace Prize (United Cultural Convention), and an Aerospace Excellence Award (Civil Air Patrol), just to name a few.

Marlene's youth program with the show, "Turn It Around, Compliment Bound" (www.UBUbound.com) is an established business. It helps mentor young people to take whatever has happened to them, learn from these experiences, and move forward. She offers tools to be successful in areas from financial to thinking outside the box. Her main platform is "UP".

Her newest project (www.marlenegrace.com) is about empowering people who have lost loved ones, especially a spouse. Marlene says, "Taxes and death are unavoidable, therefore we must be fully prepared when the time comes."

To find out more: www.MarleneGrace.com & www.UBUbound.com & (801) 791-7630

What personal event or universal problem made you want to do what you do?

When I was five years old (just before my sixth birthday), my father, who was a doctor and had heart problems, passed away. When I was born, he was going to university, so my parents had put off having more babies. They were just getting ready to have more babies when he passed away. So, I grew up as an only child and as the center of my mother's life. Because of this, I've always had an involvement with life-and-death issues and was also concerned about one-parent families. There weren't many one-parent families when I was growing up, but it's very common now. There are many people, especially baby boomers, who have lost family members so a large part of what I do is help people cope with the loss of a loved one.

What has been the hardest part of doing what you do?

I have a lot of empathy and insight, because of my personal experiences, so I teach at schools and work with teenagers frequently. I was pretty small when I went to high school myself; I had actually stopped growing for two years because of the shock of my father's passing. Being the smallest in high school was interesting as I looked like I was still in elementary school. I've seen and worked with a lot of teenagers, many who have even committed suicide. I've had to be the one to tell classmates that one of their friends is no longer with us. That's really tough. I want to do programs that empower young people so they have hope for the future.

What keeps you going when things are tough?

What keeps me going is humor. I love the theater and I take laughter's last stand! The most important thing about comedy is timing, and that produces humor. Getting through life with a smile, when things are really tough, and saying, "Well, this is all material for the book!" really helps.

What's been the most rewarding part of what you do?

Getting people to live and find their potential. I love putting people on pedestals and helping them empower themselves. My program, You Be You, teaches being the best you can be. We do that with theater, writing, art, and schoolwork. There are many opportunities out there. We live in a negative society. We want young people to have realistic goals and still know that the sky's the limit and opportunities are limitless.

The students who really benefit from my You Be You program go on to do a program called Turn it Around Compliment Bound, where we actually do artwork and writing, and combine the left and right brain. The young people who are struggling really get it, and it gives them a lot of hope. The young people who are gifted, and who get bored in school, love it because it gives them a new creative outlet.

My mission is: I create. I love to create whatever we create. We create our joy, our happiness, and our ability to cope with whatever's going on. I've worked with teenagers who have had brothers or sisters who have been killed in car accidents, and it's really rewarding to help them get through that.

What is the most inspiring transformation or manifestation that you've witnessed in your work?

We're working with life and death on many, many levels. The key is that you can live your life to the fullest—that you can be you, be yourself, be who you're meant to be, be empowered—and create the life that you want to create.

I play a character named Scarlet O'Airhead, and I go into art classes, English classes, and counseling classes to help students determine their careers, especially with junior high school age. I dress up and say, "Now, your teacher told me when I finish talkin' to y'all that I have to have a really good close, so I bought this dress and I hope y'all like it." I play with turning the words around with funny things like that. I say that it doesn't matter what happened to them, but I have two rules; one is that I don't accept anything crude, rude, or obscene, and the second rule is we have fun. I tell them, "You'll forget a lot of things you did in school, but you'll never forget Miss Scarlet coming to school. If you don't want to stay in the classroom, you can go to another room and do your other schoolwork." I've never had anybody leave.

I do a lot of programs in junior high, because I figure that junior high, the middle school age, is a really forgotten area. There are lots of programs for children, high school, and adults, but not for middle schoolers. In my art class, they come up with things like, "In my hot chocolate, you are the marshmallows," and other really fun metaphors, and they draw the picture of the steaming hot chocolate with the marshmallows popping up. Or, they might say, "In my can of pop, you're the fizz," or "You make my time tick"—fun things like that. We put up compliments and use the humor for put-ups rather than put-downs. I gathered the work from one particular art class and noticed there were over 30 pictures by the same artist. There was no name on most of them, but I realized this project was suddenly therapy. Children who are struggling don't just do one picture; they do many pictures.

When I teach a class, I say, "It doesn't matter what's happened to you. You can get through this. We can put it up." They called Einstein an idiot and he became Man of the Century. So I say, "If anybody ever calls you an idiot, you can say, 'I'm on the path to genius.'"

On one paper, I noticed, a girl had drawn a knight in one place and said, "If I was a knight, you'd be my armor," and some really beautiful metaphors. I said to the teacher, "I really feel this work is therapy." By the time I returned to teach the next class, this little girl was gone. Her mother had died of cancer and her father had committed suicide the Saturday before my class. Social services had taken the girl out of the home because she had to take care of her little brother. I had provided therapy to help her get through that situation. I, of course, had no idea what ever became of her, but I was really grateful I had been there for her that day. I know I've helped other children.

One day, I had a particular English class. Their parents were drug addicts and alcoholics. The teacher said it was her worst class. We started the class and I took them to another planet, where we drank the water, put on our oxygen, did our brain gym, cross crawl, and linked the right and left brain together. I told them that whatever problems they had were left behind on Earth and we were there to create. At the end of the class, the students gathered around me and said they had so much fun.

The teacher said, "I cannot believe this! This is such a tough class. Some of this artwork they did was phenomenal. I want you do to that for all the classes."

As I taught them, whatever happened, we turned around and put things up. That was a pretty profound experience, to realize something so easy, but when you're a teenager, you don't realize how profound an effect something like that can have.

Shortly before my mother passed away, there was an Indian boy in British Columbia who was around 12 years old.

He jumped off the Pattullo Bridge and my mom said to me, "Your program's not working."

I said, "Mom, my program *is* working, but it needs to work; it needs to get out there."

I think of my mom's words often, and I know it's really important that we contact teenagers because sometimes they don't have a lot of friends and if you can be the one person for them, it will make a difference in their lives. That's what it's about—being that one person that can be there to help.

History repeats itself and now I'm a new widow so, again, I'm dealing with life and death. My husband, who was only 58 years old, had a heart attack. I'm creating a new program to empower teenagers and young people as well as widows and widowers. I've also started a new website to help widows: www.MarleneGrace.com. We're dealing things that you might not think of when you lose a spouse and forming a community to support you as you get through this initial shock, because it is a shock to your system. We can help you turn it around.

Bradlee Snow

"It's amazing how the Universe brings about all the little things I need to go further and open my eyes to what else is possible, to how much bigger this can get."

Bradlee Snow is an author, a speaker, and an animal advocate. She's a person of many enthusiasms, but none more vital to her than animal welfare and humane education. Among her many roles, she has worked with veterinarians, and volunteers her time with animal welfare organizations such as SPCA Los Angeles. She also worked for The Walt Disney Company for over 17 years.

Bradlee believes that most children are naturally compassionate toward animals. She recognized that, in order to eliminate instances of abuse by adults, a child's natural compassion needs to be nurtured and empowered. This is what inspired Bradlee to write her best-selling book, *Jack the Cat: An Angel's Tale*. The story encourages children's natural compassion toward animals and provides suggestions of activities that empower children to become advocates for animals, even at an early age.

Bradlee trained with Peak Potentials (one of the largest personal development training companies in the world) for four years to become a world class trainer and a voice for animals worldwide. Her compassionate nature, coupled with her passion for her vision, has children engaged, inspired and motivated to take action on behalf of all animals.

To find out more: www.JackTheCatAngel.com & mbsnow@msn.com & (562) 354-7566

What personal event or universal problem made you want to do what you do?

I've been very touched by ads and news stories that I've seen, of unspeakable abuse to animals. I see the pictures and the looks in their eyes, and I'm aware of how very responsible we humans are for caring for the planet. We've been given a great responsibility to care for all life forms, and we've been given a lot of special gifts to do that. We've lost sight of this in some ways. It's been an evolution to "man up," if you will, to that responsibility.

I'm not sure where this coldness toward animals comes from. The inability to recognize the sentience of all life forms has been erased from today's modern society, and it hurts my heart to see the suffering. Because I volunteer at the shelter, I see it. It's incredible to me that people can treat creatures, who have no purpose other than to live their lives and do what they do, so cruelly; we disrespect them by being cruel to them, and negligent in their care.

I feel it's the children who are going to make the difference. We have to train them to be aware and to recognize that they *can* make a difference… that they can do things…that they have to know the difference.

What has been the hardest part of doing what you do?

The hardest part has been figuring out how to, first of all, communicate that to children and also, to be perfectly blunt, how to make a living doing it! It's all well and good to help out with charities—which I gladly and openly do on a regular basis—however, you have to *have* money in order to *give* money, and having an income makes it possible for you to spend the time giving. My biggest challenge was trying to figure out how to do, and have, both the time and the ability to make that giving possible.

What keeps you going when things are tough?

What keeps me going is volunteering, being with the animals, seeing how they come in (they are so badly cared for if they've been running loose or dropped off by their owners or abandoned), and working with them to comfort them and make a difference in allaying their fears.

Also, my cat, Jack, stares at me. I look in his eyes and he somehow speaks to my heart and keeps me going.

He says, "You've got to do this. We matter."

That's how I get re-energized.

What's been the most rewarding part of what you do?

The most rewarding part has been seeing how calm dogs and cats can become, simply by giving them the attention they need, and talking with children, who come into the shelter, and seeing them learn to be respectful and to look at the animals with a whole different perspective.

When you explain to them, "This dog has feelings, and if you run up to it really fast, you're going to frighten it, so you need to be calmer," they get it immediately!

They get it because they look in the animals' eyes, and, basically, they see other children, because animals often have bigger eyes and small, rounded faces. Animals communicate in their own little ways and children get that very clearly.

As I've been going forward teaching this, I have learned so much about the relationships people have with animals. The variety is quite fascinating. It's rewarding to reach people, and fun to see what happens as we evolve.

What is the most inspiring transformation or manifestation that you've witnessed in your work?

First of all, in talking with people about what I'm doing, and the project with my book, they've read my words and they suddenly realize, "Gosh, I've been negligent! I realize now, as much as I say I love my pets, I've let them go with their water dish empty."

Seeing how they become more responsible, and more aware, has been very rewarding and it keeps me thinking: *All right! This is the right path! This is what we're doing—just making people aware!*

What also keep me going are the amazing opportunities that have manifested themselves just by my making this commitment to get the word out, go with my heart, and follow my purpose. It's amazing how the Universe brings about all the little things I need to go further and open my eyes to what else is possible, to how much bigger this can get. It's an amazing journey, and I feel like I've only just begun. It's really going to be exciting to see where this goes!

Amy Todisco

"I can see and feel a world where the water, air, soil, and food are clean and healthy. People, everywhere, have enough energy to live comfortably."

Amy Todisco is a green living expert, green consultant, writer and life coach. Amy began her work as a community activist in 1995, and has created community educational events, founded and co-founded several nonprofits, served as Executive Director for two nonprofits, provided presentations on household toxics, and consulted with private and public schools, churches, community groups, local boards of health, and the MA State Department of Public Health. She has written, on the topic of household toxics, for newspapers, newsletters, and websites, and has been interviewed on TV and radio.

Amy has been featured on Vermont Public Television and WCAX-TV in Burlington, Vermont, was contacted by a producer from "The Oprah Winfrey Show," interviewed for an online article for www.FoxNews.com, interviewed for a Rachel Ray magazine article, and has been featured in numerous magazines, including *Vermont Life* and *Farm&Ranch*. She served as the technical editor for the *Green Living for Dummies* book.

What grew out of a desire to find the safest, most environmentally friendly lifestyle choices for her family, blossomed into a full-blown passion. She has become the voice for those who are looking for a truly organic and natural way of life.

To find out more: www.GreenLivingNow.com & amy@greenlivingnow.com

What personal event or universal problem made you want to do what you do?

I grew up on the Upper East Side of Manhattan in the 1970s. Not a great time to live there, even if you like cities, which I don't. I am someone who is profoundly impacted by my environment. The police sirens, the concrete, the dirt, the scary people…it was all very overwhelming.

One of my coping mechanisms was to watch "Little House on The Prairie" and "The Waltons" on TV. I believed that if—no, *when*—I lived in the country, I'd run through the beautiful mountain fields and pastures and breathe the fresh air. I'd eat my homegrown organic food, play with my dogs, cats, and horses, drink clean water, sleep to the sound of crickets, and be a much happier, healthier person, overall.

Before I got to Vermont, I lived in Massachusetts for about 20 years after college, most of that time in Marblehead. It was a lovely seacoast community, but all I could see was the coal-fired power plant next door and the resulting black soot on everything. Then there were all the tiny, postage stamp-sized lawns with those blazing yellow warning flags from pesticide applications. Poison…danger…yuck.

In 1992, I became pregnant. I set out to be the healthiest pregnant mom-to-be I could. That was until I found the tiny little paperback book, *The Nontoxic Baby*. That book changed my life. I learned that I was inadvertently bringing toxic chemicals into my home and into my body, and potentially my baby, via everyday household products, such as shampoo, cleaning detergents, carpets, paints, food, and more.

How was it that manufacturers were allowed to use toxic synthetic chemicals, even in products intended for babies and young children? Wasn't someone, or some entity, supposed to be protecting us, making us safe? Apparently not. So, it seemed it was up to me to research and find the products and practices that truly were safer and healthier. Not an easy task, but once I made the changes in my own home, I couldn't help but share them far and wide with others.

What has been the hardest part of doing what you do?

There are two things, really. When I was creating the original Marblehead EarthFest, forming the Marblehead Cancer Prevention Project (MCPP), and working with the Board of Health to implement new guidelines for homeowner pesticide use, I felt like I had really stepped into my power. I was doing something that was making a difference…something that could profoundly, positively impact people's lives. And, I had this wonderful little easygoing child I dragged around with me to meetings. It was really exciting. That was until I noticed that a couple of women were trying to claim ownership and take credit for my ideas and hard work. One actually told me she was jealous that I had created the Earth Day event, and that it should have been her idea. This blew my mind. So, I told her and her husband to create the opening ceremony. The other woman went around doing public speaking events, talking to the media, and generally trying to claim that she was the sole founder of the nonprofit that I had started to address and educate people about the potential environmental causes of the high cancer rates in the town. What should have been one of the proudest moments in my life turned out to be rather bittersweet, especially because no one who knew the truth was really willing to stand up for me. Looking back, I realized right then and there that it was safer to do big things for other people and their businesses than to do them for myself, because people were less likely to take credit for my work, and more likely to positively acknowledge me for my efforts. Thankfully, now I have lots of wonderful, supportive people in my life, who acknowledge my creativity and hard work, and I'm stepping back into my own power.

The second thing was trying to figure out which companies to trust, now more than ever, to tell us the truth about what's in their products. I used to think shopping in a natural food store guaranteed me that the products sold there were screened by someone and found to be safer and healthier. Not so. Sadly, some products were very similar to supermarket brands with a few extra herbs thrown in and nice, earthy-looking packaging. Some products blatantly lied, claiming to be nontoxic, earth friendly, and biodegradable while still using toxic chemical dyes, neurotoxins, and other nasty stuff.

Unfortunately, our labeling laws are inadequate. Manufacturers aren't even required to tell us exactly what's in our cleaning products.

About ten years ago, I created a nonprofit that would hire toxicologists to test the household products that were marketed as "nontoxic" and "natural" to see which ones really were. Then I'd have some science behind what I knew to be true. Unfortunately, funding wasn't easy to get back then, and we couldn't raise enough money to do the testing. So, researching was a bit more challenging, but not impossible.

What keeps you going when things are tough?

I can see and feel a world where the water, air, soil, and food are clean and healthy. People, everywhere, have enough energy to live comfortably. We all practice preventative health care instead of the "pop a pill" mentality promoted by many in the health care industry.

Before my daughter was born, I found this amazing coloring book, in a natural food store in Massachusetts, which depicted a healthy, environmentally sustainable world. I colored the whole thing and took out each page and taped it to her wall in one long line. It was so inspiring.

I think part of my life purpose and passion is to help bring that world into reality.

What's been the most rewarding part of what you do?

I love hearing from people whose lives I've positively touched with the information I've shared or a product I've sold them, especially when it improves their health.

Even though my environmental activism experiences in Marblehead were bittersweet, I'm still tremendously proud of what I brought to that community, the eyes I opened, and the people I mobilized to make change.

One of the most amusing memories I have from my Marblehead experiences is when I wrote a letter to the editor, encouraging people to do their own research about vaccinating their children. I gave the other side of the story about the potential dangers and risks. One of my friends took her new baby to a local pediatrician and asked him about the dangers of vaccinating. She told me that he almost climbed onto his desk, turned red, and started sputtering about some Amy Todisco, who was scaring people about vaccinating their children. If just asking a question could bring about that kind of response, I knew I was on to something.

What is the most inspiring transformation or manifestation that you've witnessed in your work?

While I have loved getting positive feedback from strangers whom I've reached and inspired, the most inspiring is watching what has happened to the three people closest to me.

My fabulous and healthy daughter, Diana, is 19 and never needed an antibiotic while she was growing up. She only got approximately two colds per year. She was raised on an organic whole foods diet, nontoxic household products, relatively fresh air (once we moved to Vermont), and outdoor exercise.

My ex-husband, Paul, when I met him, ate the average American diet. He used to get bronchitis regularly, but not after he switched over to our nontoxic lifestyle. And even though we are no longer together, he still reads product labels, eats organic food, recycles and is much more conscious of the choices he makes.

My current partner, Dave, never slept until I met him. His diet wasn't particularly healthy, either, even though he's an organic farmer, because he worked ridiculous hours during the growing season and often even skipped meals due to lack of time. Since we've been together, he's eaten really well, found that he was finally able to sleep, has done acupuncture, been to the chiropractor, gotten massage, uses essential oils, and his overall health and vitality have improved.

What all of this tells me is that the three people closest to me (and me, too) have been thriving as a result of this lifestyle, and that truly inspires me and keeps me going.

Rudy Milanovich

*"There is a certain feeling of freedom in getting to do
what you love as your business."*

Rudy Milanovich is a director, producer, cinematographer, and editor for television in Hollywood, California. He moved to California in July of 1998 to follow his dream of working in television. When he arrived, Rudy was hired, almost immediately, at a production facility by Keith Leon. They quickly became best friends and eventually left the production facility to start their own production company.

Since being hired as director for "The John Kerwin Show"—a national television show that airs on JLTV (Jewish Life Television), YouTube, and www.TheJohnKerwinShow.com—Rudy has had the pleasure of directing actors and performers, including Ed Asner, Cloris Leachman, Brian McKnight, Tom Bergeron, Steve Wozniak, Eric Roberts, Sean Young, Michael Dorn, Nancy Cartwright, and Bruce Dern.

Rudy is the proud owner of Wizard Vision Productions. His passion is in cinematography and directing. He honed his skills in television, working on various projects, press kits, video news releases, and actor reels before landing major clients, such as The Walt Disney Company, Warner Brothers, On the Scene Productions, Agape Media International, and Paul Ryan Productions.

Although he's a seasoned veteran in television, Rudy looks forward to moving his skills to film in the near future.

Rudy is also a very skilled and talented book layout artist. If your manuscript has been edited and you're ready to turn it into a book, call Rudy. His prices are competitive and the quality of his work is unsurpassed.

To find out more: rudy@wizardvision.net & (310) 908-9700

What personal event or universal problem made you want to do what you do?

In 1986, I read a book called, *The Nine Faces of Christ*, by Dr. Eugene Whitworth. That book changed my life because it is the very thing that awakened me, spiritually. For me, it put into perspective God, religion, and my relationship with both of them. The book helped me to realize that God is something within me, not something outside of me or something I need to spend the rest of my life searching for. I always felt that the book would make a great movie.

Soon after completing the book, I was attending a spiritual event and the speaker was talking about how to know if you are doing what you are supposed to be doing in life. When the speaker said, "Don't you know that your dreams are your plans?" a light bulb went off in my head. I realized that all I ever wanted to do was work in Hollywood, in some capacity, so I packed my bags and moved from New Mexico to California with the ultimate dream of making the film.

When I moved to California, I had four friends who already lived there. One of my friends said I could stay with her until I got on my feet. In one of our many conversations as roommates, I mentioned my dream of making a film based on the book that had changed my life. My roommate informed me that she had a friend who knew Dr. Whitworth, and gave me her friend's number. I called her friend and shared my compelling story with him. He ended up giving me Dr. Whitworth's phone number. I called Dr. Whitworth on New Year's Day 1999. Surprisingly, he answered the phone.

When I explained why I was calling and shared my big dream with him, he said, "Great, let's meet in person."

We set a date and time and, a few months later, I found myself sitting in his office. He hired me, that day, to shoot a documentary for him in Mexico based on another book he had written. Dr. Whitworth and I formed a friendship that lasted until he passed away in December of 2004. He gave me permission to do the film and I have every intention of making that film in the future. Meeting him was truly a blessing in my life.

What has been the hardest part of doing what you do?

The hardest part has been breaking into the inner circle of Hollywood and the unions. Doing something I love has been relatively easy for me, but doing it on a bigger scale has been a challenge.

What keeps you going when things are tough?

I absolutely love what I do and not many people can say that. I look forward to doing it every day. It feels like I'm on a perpetual vacation; it never feels like work and it's never something I "have" to do. There is a certain feeling of freedom in getting to do what you love as your business.

When times are tough, I operate on faith. I have learned, in the past, that no matter how bad things appear to be on the outside, it's only a matter of time before it will become positive. I just do my best to remember that, when things appear to be out of alignment in my business life or personal life.

What's been the most rewarding part of what you do?

The most rewarding part is being a part of something creative. I never thought of myself as being very creative and working in television has really opened me up to my own creativity. Not only have I been directing "The John Kerwin Show," but I edited the show for years. It was incredibly rewarding to put together a full hour show and have it come together seamlessly. While working on each show, I love to see all of the audience members laughing and having a great time, and then to have them come up, after the show, and say things like, "This is the best TV show I have seen in person, and I've been to some pretty well-known shows," is really great, too. Being able to do what I love, and be of service at the same time, is extremely gratifying.

I feel so blessed by some of the people I've had the pleasure of working with in my career. The first person who comes to mind is Dr. Robert Young. He wrote a book called, The pH Miracle, which I read several years ago and it changed my life. Then I got to meet and work with him at his ranch in San Diego for a week. That was pretty amazing.

Another truly inspiring meeting was Arun Gandhi, the grandson of Mahatma Gandhi. I got to shoot an interview with him. It was uplifting and enlightening.

I also had the pleasure to work with Burt Reynolds, who has been one of my favorite actors since childhood. That was one of my dreams actualized.

What is the most inspiring transformation or manifestation that you've witnessed in your work?

The most inspiring transformation I've witnessed, in many years, has actually been within myself and who I have become since the birth of my granddaughter, Mckena. The birth wasn't planned and I had judgment on my stepdaughter. I judged her for being too young, for poor planning, for not being set up financially—all the usual stuff. Ultimately, the only thing my judgment of my stepdaughter had done was create a distance between my granddaughter and me. I hadn't gotten to know her at all and before I knew it, two years had gone by.

After Mckena turned two years old, I began to play with her when she'd come over to our house. She would allow me to play with her but, ultimately, at some point she would call out for her grandma as if she had had enough of me. I couldn't blame her as I hadn't been exactly been warm and fuzzy with her for her first two years of life.

One day, when she was about two and a half years old, I was playing with her in our backyard and she looked at me and said, "Let's go for a walk, Grandpa."

I was not only shocked by her request but a little scared. You see, I had never been alone with her (without her grandma or her parents around).

I said, "Okay," and we started walking.

I thought it would be a five- to ten-minute walk but as we were walking, I found a path and asked her if she wanted us to take it.

She said, "Yes."

At the end of the path, we found a park that neither one of us knew was there and we ended up spending the next three hours in the park playing on the swings, sliding on the slides, and swinging on the monkey bars. She didn't want to leave this great place we had discovered together. It was like we had found her personal Heaven. By the time we left, we were worn out. I ended up carrying her home and she fell asleep in my arms with her head on my shoulder. That was the single greatest day of my life and since that day, Mckena and I have been the best of friends. We continue to go to that same park, at least once a week, and she always wants to come along whenever grandpa goes somewhere. She has even visited me at work and been on one of our television broadcasts. She is the light of my life, along with my wife, Nida, and I am grateful for each and every moment we spend together.

Marjean Holden

*"My mission is to touch, move, and inspire people
to live in their purpose with passion and power."*

Marjean Holden is a very successful international transformational trainer, speaker, actress, producer, stuntwoman, and mom—a woman who is extremely passionate about inspiring and encouraging others to dream bigger, express themselves more fully, and have more freedom in their lives.

In 2005, after starring or appearing in over 40 feature films and television shows, Marjean put her successful twenty-plus year acting career in the entertainment industry on hold to pursue another of her lifelong dreams of inspiring others from the personal development platform.

Two years prior, in 2003, Marjean had been introduced to Peak Potentials, T. HarvEker's success training company. At Peak Potentials Marjean discovered an organization whose mission, of educating and inspiring people to live in their higher selves, was in alignment with her own. She subsequently became Peak Potentials' first female trainer, then expanded into leading T. Harv Eker Signature programs in Singapore, Malaysia, the UK, Italy, Germany, Holland, Australia, and Taiwan.

Though Marjean continues to travel the globe, training and facilitating people to break through their limitations and attain new levels of success in their lives, she has now stepped back into the film industry, where she will not only be in front of the camera again, but also behind it as a writer and producer. So far, she has helped transform the lives of tens of thousands of people from around the globe and is ready to broaden her horizons and take her message to the world through the magic of movies.

To find out more: www.MarjeanHolden.com

What personal event or universal problem made you want to do what you do?

The personal event that happened was…I was born! When I was really young, I used to think: *What is it that people want most?* I don't know why, but I thought all the time, as a kid, about how I wanted to fulfill my dreams. I was around so many people who did what they had to do to get by, who didn't love their work. I saw it over and over again. I determined when I was in high school: *That's not going to be me. I'm going to do what I love. I'm going to do what makes me happy, what's in my heart. I know there's a way it will happen. I'll be financially able to support myself and be as rich as I want.* Granted, there were some jobs that, because I came from the entertainment industry, I would take because I needed the job to take care of everything, but I was still doing what I loved doing, which was acting. From acting, I knew that I could make a difference in the world by helping people to follow their dreams. I knew that even if they were doing something they didn't want to be doing, they could do what was in their hearts and their dreams, part-time, so they had something to look forward to while they were taking care of everything they needed, until they had the courage to step out and go full-on into what their heart said and what made them really happy.

That's something that has always been really clear to me; some people in the world do things because they have to or they need to, and not necessarily because they desire or want to. My mission is to touch, move, and inspire people to live in their purpose with passion and power. The only way I can do that is if I'm living in my purpose with passion and power. Everything I do comes from my heart and makes me happy. I think that's really important.

What has been the hardest part of doing what you do?

There are two different facets, and I'll talk about the entertainment industry first. The hardest part about the entertainment industry has been developing thick skin to hear the word, "No. No. No." It's a numbers game, an odds game, until you get to the level that you're an A-lister and they're calling for you. I was never at that level; I was always at auditions and casting people would bring me in over and over again. Even though I worked with some producers more than once, and others over and over again, I kept hearing the word "no." Coming into the philosophies and principles of the Law of Attraction, I learned that the answer is always "yes" to whatever question you're asking. I began working those principles. I found personal development when I was acting, so I did a lot of work on myself when I was in the acting industry. It helped me stay grounded, centered, and focused, in conjunction with the thought that: *This is my career and what I love to do, but I know I can stay happy and stay grounded, even if I don't get that job or that big movie or whatever it is.* Was I still doing what I loved? Absolutely. Could I help other people do what they loved? Absolutely. Hearing "no" was one of the hardest things for me until I thought: *I'm going to keep moving forward.* I had a great career as an actress. I heard "yes" a lot more than a *lot* of people have ever heard yes.

There were two difficult things about going into personal development. The hardest part—after I decided that I wanted to actually teach and train in personal development—was that it was brand new for me. I had no idea what training was. I had done a few sitcoms in front of a live audience, but the majority of my career had been film and television. Film is never done in front of a live audience. Getting on the personal development stage, being authentic, being myself, and being totally transparent—when I'm really quite a private person—was one of the hardest things for me. You just have to be transparent. Just be who you are. Let them know all the hardships, the struggles, and everything that you've gone through. Allowing myself to be vulnerable in front of thousands of people, I thought: *Whoa! Now they know that about me and it's okay.*

The second tough part, for me, is that the training industry is male-dominated; there are a lot more men in the business than there are women in the business. I don't know why that is, it just is. One of the biggest challenges has been staying in my power in the feminine, as opposed to going into the masculine energy. I had to learn and study more of the feminine principles and energy, and the goddess energy, in order to stand in my truth as a woman, understanding fully that there is that masculine part of me and I can run that energy, but that's also a place where running that energy leads to burnout, which I've suffered. Having to go back into a more gentle feminine flow with creativity—as opposed to just *do, do, do, do, do*—that's been difficult.

What keeps you going when things are tough?

I go to the spa! Seriously, however, when things are tough, I always revert back to my girlfriends—my feminine support system—and some men who understand that feminine energy, and can fill me back up. There are one or two people, in particular, who would just be there for me, hands down, no matter what's going on in my life. They've known me for so long, they just know, "This is what you need right now, so let's go do that." Other times, I'll just hibernate and ask: *What does Marjean need to do for Marjean? What would be fun for me right now? What would make me happy right now?* I'm a big advocate of playing, having fun, and doing things that I loved to do when I was a kid. When things are really tough, I try to lighten myself up. I can be very intense with myself, so I try to lighten up. I love reading fantasy and science fiction. I'll cuddle up with a cup of tea, or I'll go watch movies. Because I'm in the entertainment industry, movies are a huge outlet for me to bring myself back into center. It reminds me: *I've got this creative streak in me; let me go watch something that makes me happy.* Or, I go and get on a horse and ride!

What's been the most rewarding part of what you do?

I'd have to say the most rewarding part of everything I've done in my life is seeing when the light goes on for someone. Especially in the training industry, but even in the film industry when I was on the set and I had an opportunity, people would open up to me and I would give them some sort of wisdom or something that would help them move through. There's nothing greater than having someone come back to me a year, two years, or five years after I've talked to them, seen them, or had an opportunity to train them, and come back saying, "You changed my life. What you said to me changed my life." Nine times out of ten, I won't remember what I said to them, because I let Spirit move through me in the moment, and I let whatever they need to hear in that moment come out. I usually don't remember because it's not me consciously doing it; it's a Higher Power. I've learned to be open to the messages, to let them come out when they need to come out, and just facilitate that.

I've been fortunate to train people all over the world since 2009. I recently had a gentleman from Italy come up to me and say, "You know, you are the only woman who's ever transformed my life. Not even my wife." It has been really powerful to see the impact that I've had on my students, the men in particular, by giving them the space to be open, to allow them to see themselves in a different way. It's true for the women as well, helping women stand in their power and be proud of who they are. For the men, it gets back into being a man with feelings who cares, loves, and is a powerful, strong leader. To be able to stand in front of a man who's in his fifties or sixties, and have him look at me and cry and say, "I didn't love myself until I worked with you. You taught me how to love myself." That, to me, is the best thing. Then to have people in the film industry come up to me and ask, "When are you doing another event? I really want to work with you. I loved working with you." It's a great feeling to leave such an impact that someone comes up to me 10 or 15 years later and says, "We've got to work together. I have to work for you." It's so rewarding, so fulfilling, and just makes my heart sing.

What is the most inspiring transformation or manifestation that you've witnessed in your work?

I get so inspired by the courage I see in my students when I'm teaching. Some of them have been through so much.

Here's an example. We deal with racism here in America and all over the world. I had one student last year, from an Asian country, who, after I took her class through a process, said to me, "I was always racist until this activity, until this process. Now I can see people as spirit and as love and energy, no matter where they're from." I thought: *Whoa, that is huge. That is powerful—so powerful.* To see that occurring, in every culture I teach, has been so inspiring in my own life and so transforming to know I had a part in it. For people who have physical limitations to come through, and to do everything that they do...the strength of Spirit that I see in them makes me realize that life is good...life is *so* good.

Doing the personal development and training has given me more opportunity to explore myself and where I would consider a "weakness" in myself. I know there are no weaknesses; there are things that are empowering or disempowering. I see where I have disempowering beliefs, and to transform them is not always easy, of course. But it's great just to have that opportunity—and the reflection of my students is fantastic.

Business Support

Susanne Hopfner

*"It takes dedication to navigate the waters of business life.
Every day brings a new challenge, and I'm ready for it."*

Susanne Hopfner is a virtual assistant and founder of edos, a document, office service, and virtual assistant company located in the foothills of the Great Dividing Range of the Northern Rivers Region in NSW, Australia. The edos suite of services provides a platform to assist a broad range of clients both in regional Australia as well as metropolitan areas and international locations.

Born in Germany, Susanne came to Australia two decades ago. Her work ethic and high quality standards enabled a successful career in both private and public sector organizations in business support and human resource service areas. Susanne is passionate about lifelong learning.

edos operates 100 percent on solar energy and has a very low ecological footprint.

Susanne's and the edos' vision is to deliver services that foster positive and effective communication for people in their private or business lives.

To find out more: www.edosOnlineServices.com &
susanne.hopfner@bigpond.com

What personal event or universal problem made you want to do what you do?

A few years ago, my husband and I traded the urban landscapes of Brisbane, Australia for a place in the Australian bush and became "tree changers." The lure of a more self-sustainable lifestyle, being in a more natural environment, and the real prospect of decreasing our ecological footprint was irresistible. So, in 2005, we packed up and moved to our new home on a mountain top.

Bush life can be challenging, especially when it comes to finding work in an office, which is how I had spent the last 30 odd years of my working career. The area we moved to has a high rate of unemployment when compared to the national average. I had applied for about a dozen jobs in my field of work, prior to relocating, and was unsuccessful in gaining any of the positions for which I was interviewed. Furthermore, the tyranny of distance can make holding down a job in the next regional centre a sobering experience. Now that I lived about 90 kilometers away from a potential employer, the thought of commuting two hours, minimum, by car each day made any job in town appear even less attractive and at odds with my desire to live sustainably. What was the point of moving to the country for a lifestyle change if you spend most of your time on the road and working in the next town?

That's when I remembered a dream I had about 25 years ago. On my first trip to the Australian bush, I thought that it would be just fantastic to be able to work from a bush property using the computer to bridge the geographical divide. So here I was, living in the bush now and I decided that creating my own employment was the best option. Finally, the time had come to make my dream a reality. That's how my VA business, edos (Ewingar Document & Office Services), came to life.

The national telecommunications provider had just launched the new wireless broadband network and, as luck would have it, our location on a mountain top was perfect for reception. So, I had the technological platform and began road-testing our stand-alone solar system to see if it could meet the power demands of running a business via computer all day. I was greatly relieved to find that the solar system stood up to the requirements, and I am really proud to operate a business with such a low ecological footprint.

What has been the hardest part of doing what you do?

It's difficult to pin this down to just one thing. For me it's about getting the nexus right between commitments to my business and life in general. I have seen a lot of small business owners become a slave to their business for various reasons. Having come off the treadmill of a nine-to-five job in the city, I promised myself that I wouldn't let the business run my life and exhaust my energy reserves. So, I vowed to keep my body and mind in good shape, not just to enjoy good health, but also to enable me to provide the best possible service to my clients. I am convinced that reliability and consistency in what I do, on an everyday basis, is the key to operating a successful VA business. I quickly realized that I had to be at the top of my game to be successful.

Since business and home life unfold on the same stage, this proved a little more challenging than I first thought. Working from home is considered to be the Holy Grail by many people, including myself. Doing your first job of the day in your pajamas, having a break when the dog wants to take you for a walk, starting to cook dinner early, or just stepping out into the garden to smell the roses—these were all romantic ideas about what working from home would be like.

The reality turned out to be a different shade of blue, when I realized that my clients deserved my commitment to excellence and timeliness in service delivery every day I work with them. I could be starting to do the dishes, and then the phone would ring and a client had an urgent task to attend to. Of course the dishwashing water would be cold by the time I got back to it.

I had to learn to employ the right personal development strategies that would allow me to have both the ability to be business focused and meet my client's deadlines, as well as be able to enjoy the lifestyle I am creating and knowing how to create balance. After all, I am now the captain of my ship and I really want to steer it in the direction I've mapped out.

What keeps you going when things are tough?

I have been operating my VA business for just over five years now. During this time, I have met many inspiring people through my business and association with the VA Placement network that I joined in late 2008. I also draw a lot of inspiration from the satisfaction of receiving positive feedback from my clients. When they tell me that I've helped them achieve their objectives, it gives me such a lift.

When things are a bit tough, I remind myself why I have gone down this path and go back in my mind to the feeling of excitement when I was "singing in the business," sitting on the carport, and waiting to get my first few clients on board. I also revisit my client success stories and reinvigorate my determination to do well for my clients. It helps me remember that what I do makes a difference in someone's life.

One of my quiet achievements was a 21st century Sherlock Holmes style investigation to help a client track down a person he'd last spoken to over 15 years ago. My client thought this person could be instrumental in providing supporting evidence for a workers' compensation claim which my client was pursuing. I was able to trace the person's contact details (it wasn't as easy as you might think, despite having online white pages and directories at my fingertips these days) which, eventually, led to a successful and substantial settlement for my client. One day, out of the blue, this client turned up on my doorstep with the prettiest potted plant and a thank you card for the help I'd given him. How could I not be bowled over and energized by this show of appreciation?

What's been the most rewarding part of what you do?

Aside from positive feedback from my clients, I have gained a new appreciation for what it means to live authentically. In my previous employment in a large organization, I felt so disenchanted that the leadership of the organization would espouse certain organizational values but came up short when living them. I could see how people, in many sections of the organization, were saying one thing and doing another.

So, in the first few months of research and setting up the business, I undertook a strategic planning exercise to think about my vision for the business and define the values that I wanted to live through my business. This is what I came up with as my values:

- Respect and fairness in all dealings
- Maintain confidentiality and privacy laws
- Honesty and integrity in all interactions
- Community focus and value for money
- Lifelong learning principles and pursuit of excellence

There has been more than one occasion when I was faced with making a difficult business decision and all I had to do was look at my values and make sure the decision was congruent. It is the most rewarding feeling when you can live your own values authentically. For me, this includes applying my business skills, not just in the pursuit of making a living, but also to help build capacity in the community in which I live.

I have supported our local community hall committee for a few years now, obtained a substantial grant payment for refurbishment work of the hall, and, more recently, wrote and delivered a deputation speech to our local Council in support of Notice of Motion against coal seam gas mining.

Another rewarding aspect of operating my VA business is that I can take the business on the road. Having a mobile Internet connection equals high flexibility. This kind of business setup allows me to participate in special events, like conferences or meeting up with friends in a holiday resort, and still be able to deliver services to my clients, if required.

What is the most inspiring transformation or manifestation that you've witnessed in your work?

As it's been such a steep learning curve for me, I struggle to single out any one of the transformations and manifestations I've seen and experienced. There have been so many. At a personal level, I think I have grown from a "rookie" to a semi-experienced business operator with a bit of nous and a sense of the endless possibilities this way of life can afford. Testament to that is the fact that I have recently taken on the position of President on the Board of the Australian Association for Virtual Industry Professionals. It takes dedication to navigate the waters of business life. Every day brings a new challenge, and I'm ready for it.

I have devoured a lot of literature about how to create and operate a small business, from creating a business vision to developing a business plan and setting targets. It all sounded pretty good on paper. However, it wasn't until I put some of the strategies in place that I realized that it's not just theory; they actually work.

I recently had a wonderful manifestation which came about through the power of goal setting. Having reassessed my business plan, I decided to set a daily target for billable hours. At the end of the day when I added my hours up, I was stunned to see that they exactly matched the goal I had set, which was a 10 percent increase on my previous average. Now I'm a convert.

Being in business for yourself is truly one of the best training grounds to develop yourself and, hopefully, become a better person in the end.

Jared Allardyce

"I was taught to work hard, treat people fairly, and take pride in my work, and that's opened door after door so that I've never had to face the situation of: Do I keep going or not?"

Jared Allardyce is the owner and communication designer of Wide Web Marketing web design and internet marketing. Jared started designing websites in the mid-1990s while attending Louisiana Tech University School of Art. After graduating in Communication Design, he gained professional experience as a designer for advertising agencies, commercial printers, and website developers. With experience in all advertising mediums, he decided to focus on the Internet because of the unparalleled ability to interact and share information with targeted audiences. Jared believes in fair pricing, quality work, and ongoing service.

Wide Web Marketing's vast client list includes ArchitTrek, EvalScore®, Jack Miller's BBQ Sauce, OsmoFlex™, The Association of Concert Bands, Website Grid, and WorldConnect IPTV.

Wide Web Marketing offers full-service website design, management, and Internet marketing. They start by analyzing your current online strategy, industry, and competition in order to present you with relevant data to support their decisions in the development process. After your website is live, they'll track and analyze visitor patterns to form a strategy for managing and marketing your site through search optimization, pay-per-click ads, and e-mail marketing.

To find out more: www.WideWebMarketing.com

What personal event or universal problem made you want to do what you do?

I wouldn't say it was a universal problem that made me want to do this for a living. I was always creative when I was growing up, so I was directed into the field of art and design naturally. But, certainly, my career evolved due to one event that turned into a pattern and directed my career path.

As a designer and creative director in both printing and interactive media, I've come across the same problem each time, where creativity meets production. You can have the best ideas in the world, or a really nice presentation or design piece, yet you will always hit the limitations of the media in which you want to present them. In my first job, I would design brochures and then send the disk to the printer. Twenty questions would come back from the printer, or twenty problems about why we couldn't do this, this, this, this, and this.

As a designer, I always wanted to know, "Why? Why can't you do that?"

So I dove more into the technical side—the mix of the creativity versus the technical. I've seen that carry through, not just in print, but in web. Instead of ink and paper being the variables, you're dealing with software, programming, and the fact that there are ten different browsers and five different screen sizes in which your art or your presentation are being displayed. Those are all the same thing; it's creativity versus the technical aspects, or the production aspects, of turning your art into a message and getting it out to your audience.

What has been the hardest part of doing what you do?

The hardest part is that we have to learn a lot about each client. We have to learn their business: we have to understand their organizational structure, their profit centers, their products and services, other marketing efforts aside from the online marketing efforts we provide, and who their competitors are. It's a challenge, each time, to wrap your head around all those aspects of a business. Then the goal is to present them to the world through their web page, and market to their target audience. It takes time to learn enough about their business to create that effective message and get it out there, and then get the business owner to invest and trust the process, and trust us to guide them through it. There has to be a certain amount of trust, simply because the field that we're in advances so quickly that it's very hard to keep up with current trends for us, as well as our clients.

What keeps you going when things are tough?

It sounds like a cliché or a common answer, but faith, family, and friends are what keep me going. If you stick to your values and surround yourself with hard-working people, then *keep going* becomes the normal reaction to any situation, whether they're tough or not. I was taught to work hard, treat people fairly, and take pride in my work, and that's opened door after door so that I've never had to face the situation of: *Do I keep going or not?* And I'm still young!

What's been the most rewarding part of what you do?

The most rewarding part is seeing our clients' reactions when they finally understand what's possible through Internet marketing. There are so many moving parts that it can be challenging for us to follow this process when we're, literally, reacting to headlines, every day…to technology, what's new, what's expected of us now, and different platforms. When our clients trust in us and have the patience to see us through the entire process, then all of a sudden they start to see the leads being generated and they understand that we can get it down to a "cost per lead" formula that they can apply to their business; the light bulb comes on. At that point, it's very gratifying to know that they now understand our efforts and see the results.

What is the most inspiring transformation or manifestation that you've witnessed in your work?

I've seen a lot of businesses and individuals succeed through our efforts. Success is not always monetary; we don't create every website for profit. Some are for charities and causes, and some are a form of expression. Regardless of the purpose, we are helping people present a message to a specific audience. Seeing that communication or connection being made, between the person crafting the message and the person or group it's intended for, is always inspiring and rewarding. That propels and inspires us to do it again and again.

Susan Keeley Jeske

"Fundraising for organizations—helping those who need to be helped, at the point they really need it—is a very rewarding experience."

Susan Keeley Jeske has over 18 years of experience in sales and marketing with an MBA from the University of Chicago's Booth School of Business. In addition to owning her own internet companies to assist fund raising organizations and charities, Susan is passionate about working with start-ups and teaching others how to create additional streams of income.

You can support Susan's various charities by shopping at www.YourTravelMinder.com and www.YourCashMinder.com. To find out how your organization can participate, receive an invitation to Susan's free Making Money Online Teleseminar, or to work directly with Susan, please email your name and phone number, with your request, to: susan@yourcashminder.com

To find out more: http://Info.YourCashMinder.com

What personal event or universal problem made you want to do what you do?

The business that I have today was a very easy business to get into. It really came from seeing the downturn of the economy. I worked for a corporation—I still do—and I have a very entrepreneurial spirit. After developing businesses for my employer, I was looking to develop a business of my own, outside of the company. During the downturn of the economy, I realized how important it was for me to create this business, not only to take control of my own personal economy, but to help others do the same. I was one of the lucky ones, so to speak, in that I didn't lose my job but a lot of my friends did. Many people, who worked for the same company that I did for 20 years, were being laid off. They were top producers in the company and they were being laid off. This happened all around the country. Many people close to me lost their homes because they could not pay their mortgages. I felt helpless because I couldn't give back or help them.

So, I changed my direction and, instead of trying to make a lot of money building a product, I thought: *What can I do to empower people to help themselves—not just when they lose a job, but when they have a job? They need options.* When you have a job, you never know what's going to happen in your life where you might need an additional stream of income. Many people are comfortable; they don't think about the future, a lot of times, until the future is there. So, I came into this business of teaching people how to make money online, as an additional stream of income, because I wanted to help people around me who actually needed a little extra cash to make it to the next month.

During the same year I gave birth to my son, I had two friends who had to bury their children. For one of them, it was his four-and-a-half-year-old daughter who had brain cancer and passed away. I wanted to find a way to help them and to give to their organizations. A few thousand dollars here and there from my own account was fine but I wanted a way to help them on a regular basis. So, that's what I do; I use my web sites for fundraising, I help people develop that additional stream of income, and I help organizations help other people.

What has been the hardest part of doing what you do?

The hardest part, when I want to help people, is seeing people who *need* the help but don't *want* the help. I don't take that personally; I realize that either what I offer is not interesting to them or they're not in the space to accept help at that point. You can't help somebody who doesn't want to be helped. It's frustrating, in a sense, but they're on their own path and maybe it's a lesson they need to learn or a path they need to take for their own growth until they find their way out.

Also, I'm doing this on the side but it is like a full-time job—plus raising a two-year-old, which is a little difficult. It's about managing the time, which is actually a good thing because, in the end, I want to work *on* my businesses and not *in* my businesses. It forces me to accept the help I need and to actually work with others and the team to do what I'm doing. I've created a network of other people who want to do the same things so we can work together on projects. It's actually much more fun that way. So, in essence, the challenge of managing my time has turned into a benefit in teaching me how to work with other people.

What keeps you going when things are tough?

I want to be an example for my son. If he faces a challenge or an obstacle, I want him to keep pushing through. When things are tough, I think of my friend's daughter who passed away from brain cancer. Those are the true warriors. They have been through all of the hospitalizations, the needles and surgeries, and so many things I can't even comprehend. That's something a three-year-old or four-year-old should never have to go through. So, if things are difficult and I want to throw a pity party for myself, it makes me think: *My life is actually pretty good. I don't have anything to be really upset about.* Anything that's a challenge is a little blip in the road compared to what some of these kids with cancer—or *anyone* with a terminal disease who is fighting for their life—have gone through. I hope my son never goes through that. I want to support parents who have to go through something like that and be strong for their child. A lot of those parents can't work while their child is going through treatments and they may have to travel across the country to doctors. The organization I'm helping is called CJ's Thumbs Up Foundation (www. cjstuf.org) and that's what they do; they give these families monetary help. Sometimes it's not a good outcome but, in a small way, I'm helping them.

So, when something is hard, I get rejected or can't figure something out, I think of the other people in the world who are having a difficult time, too. Everybody has their challenges. As long as you keep a positive outlook as you're moving forward, I find that the answer usually appears.

What's been the most rewarding part of what you do?

One of the most rewarding things, for me, has been empowering other women, other people, to take control of their lifestyles and not allow anyone to tell them what their net worth is or how they should structure their lives. Fundraising for organizations—helping those who need to be helped, at the point they really need it—is a very rewarding experience as well.

For many years, I was trying to find the way to become independent. When I started this business, it was very empowering for me. Even when I hadn't generated a dollar in my business yet, I became a business owner overnight. Now I have the opportunity to help a lot of people, to generate the personal income I'm looking for, and to create the lifestyle I want—and it's not on anybody else's clock. Nobody else tells me what I'm worth, when I have to check in, or when I'm taking my vacation. It is very empowering and rewarding for me to know that I can help another person feel the same way. I can help a person: a) build a business and transition from a corporate job they hate into a life they desire, b) continue working a low-paying job they love without compromising their lifestyle, or c) replace their income after losing a job.

What is the most inspiring transformation or manifestation that you've witnessed in your work?

That's a hard one because I am fairly new in the business, but I've seen a lot of these transformations in my life. I didn't really appreciate the depth of my experience until I started thinking about it in that way. Every day is inspiring for me. I learn something new and I accept things that come my way. If there's something I just don't know how to do, I put it out into the Universe: *I don't know how to get there, but this is what I want to create. This is what I want to see.* It has been interesting how certain people and situations come into my life at certain times and I think this book is one of them! I put out a high-level visual of where I want to be, where I want to go, and who I want to help and things show up in my life every single day! I've realized that everything doesn't have to be perfect in the beginning. Take one step at a time and know that if you don't see what you need in your path right now, it *will* appear. It's happened, time and again, in my life; I don't know how I'm going to get somewhere and then, one day, the path magically appears in front of me. Maybe it had always been there and I hadn't noticed it, or maybe it just magically appeared, but it's about taking one step at a time and keeping my eyes open to accepting the information that's coming in from the Universe after I communicate my vision. I don't need to have everything figured out from the beginning; it will organically transform itself into what it needs to be as I move forward.

Maribel Jimenez

"I teach others how to create success in their lives and I know that creates a ripple effect. I feel like I am doing my part to create a better world and that is very rewarding!"

Maribel Jimenez is an international speaker, best-selling author, and marketing mentor. She is founder of Creative Solutions Consulting, the New Superwoman community, and co-founder of Bake Your Book mentoring. She works with entrepreneurs, coaches, and consultants teaching how to market successfully online and offers a variety of programs. Her passion is to help entrepreneurs share their message in a big way, through powerful online marketing strategies, and double or triple their businesses. For the past 15 years, prior to becoming an entrepreneur, she served as Business Development and Marketing Director writing successful marketing campaigns, curriculum, and training programs for multi-million dollar organizations. She's won numerous awards including the prestigious President's Award through Toyota.

To find out more: www.TheCreativeSolutions.com

What personal event or universal problem made you want to do what you do?

I've always had the desire to create a business. Even as a child when I worked in my parents' store, I imagined helping people in some way. At the time I worked with my stuffed animals, but I knew that I would be doing it for real people someday. I went the traditional path of going to school to get a degree and getting a job until I could figure it out. I began to notice my own strengths as an employee and my desire to be the best in all that I did. And then came the craving to create my own business.

Despite the tugging I felt inside, I continued to play it safe so I could get a consistent paycheck…until one day, I just couldn't do it anymore. I was faced with a "two-by-four"—a situation that called for a decision to either keep going or fly on my own and create my own business. I chose to fly. I had a deep desire to serve others through my own strengths and create my own business. So it was time to own up to that and *just do it!*

I felt the fear and did it anyway. As a start-up entrepreneur, I experienced the rough ride that gave me strength and compassion for others who were trying to do the same. I immersed myself in the tools and training to be the best I could be, so I could support others in creating strong businesses. I saw a need to help other entrepreneurs who had gifts to share but were struggling to get their gifts out into the world. I knew that I could help them launch their businesses and programs through effective marketing.

Here I am today, successfully doing what I love and serving others to create the same.

What has been the hardest part of doing what you do?

I think the hardest part of it all is recognizing that through trials come our biggest gifts of learning. Through trials, we stretch and grow to accept more in our lives. It took me a long time to learn this lesson and, of course, I still have to catch myself now. I sometimes forget that when I get a rough patch or trial, it doesn't always mean I did something wrong (although sometimes it does). Many times it's preparation for what is to come. It doesn't feel good in the moment, but there are always blessings in disguise if we look for them. Once I remind myself of this, I can shift to the lesson and not stay in the problem.

What keeps you going when things are tough?

When things are tough, I know it's time to get still and quiet and check in with my inner guidance. I've recognized that I tend to rush forward and take action quickly, but in doing so I don't always hear the guidance through my busyness. Now, I quickly go inside and access support to help me through, give me peace, and help me learn the lesson. I have also learned to get support from others through tough times. I used to think that I would be a burden if I came to others with a problem, so I often tried to face it all alone. This kept me in the problem much longer than necessary, and with that frustration came more, through the law of attraction.

What's been the most rewarding part of what you do?

The most rewarding part is being able to play a part in changing someone's life for the better. It is so gratifying to help others, whether it's business or personal. I've had many mentors who have changed my life. I am so grateful to create a business where I can do the work I love and serve others while creating abundance. I live my life fully and am surrounded by the people I love and those who inspire me. I teach others how to create success in their lives and I know that creates a ripple effect. I feel like I am doing my part to create a better world and that is *very* rewarding!

What is the most inspiring transformation or manifestation that you've witnessed in your work?

I am inspired by the clients who are willing to be vulnerable, feel the fear, and still take action. Those are the clients who manifest most rapidly. I learned, early in my teens, to be clear about what I wanted and set goals regularly. The clearer I was, the faster I manifested them. I noticed that when I didn't have clear goals, I floundered. I teach entrepreneurs to use the law of attraction and be clear about what they want, and then take inspired action to manifest it quickly. When a client really gets this, they become unstoppable!

Charlene Levine

*"The most rewarding part of what I do is finding money
for business owners and seeing the look
of relief on their faces."*

Charlene Levine powerfully entered the world of commercial lending out of necessity. Years ago, when one of Charlene's acquaintances, a small business owner, was struggling to obtain funds for business expansion and had been rejected by several lenders, Charlene agreed to use her business experience to find a funding source. At that time, she became aware of the quandary that many business owners in the U.S. face when they do not know where to turn to get loans.

Through extensive research, Charlene was able to offer her acquaintance a viable funding solution. She came to understand that often a lack of funding, for a relatively stable business, can cause bankruptcy and cessation of business activities. These losses are grave for the business owners, their employees, and the U.S. economy. Charlene realized she could use her expertise in business and training in communication to help business owners get funding that they were not otherwise able to obtain. She is passionate about helping people in business get the funding they need to fulfill on their dreams of operating and expanding profitable businesses.

Charlene and her partner, Chris Yurko, at C & C Funding, LLC, have developed a unique network of funding sources, beyond conventional banks, that can get business owners what they want and need…cash! Charlene and Chris specialize in helping business owners get funding even when they have been rejected previously, and even when they have compromised credit. In these cases, getting the necessary funds is still possible! It is so gratifying for Charlene to contribute to our society by helping businesses and business owners, the backbone of the U.S. economy.

To find out more: clevine@cwrnow.com & (248) 894-8688

What personal event or universal problem made you want to do what you do?

Several years ago, I began helping an older couple with their business and financial issues. We will call them Gladys and Bill for the purpose of this story. Gladys was 78 and Bill was 80. They owned a dance studio business that was connected to their home, and had operated the business for over 60 years. The business had flourished and served them well. They had worked very hard all their lives and, at one point, had money saved for retirement.

As time went along, however, in their efforts to help their children, Bill and Gladys overextended themselves financially. They loved their three girls and would do anything to help them and their grandchildren. I happened to be friends with one of their daughters, Susie, and knew of the family situation. At different times, Bill and Gladys' daughters and grandchildren needed money, which Gladys and Bill provided without thinking about their own future and what might happen to them. With the recession, the enrollment in their dance studio began to dwindle and they found that with their heavy debt and credit card issues, they could barely make ends meet.

With their retirement funds gone, they began borrowing money from Susie to pay for all the debt they had accumulated. This situation was embarrassing and very stressful for them—having no financial cushion and going further into debt. While they were still working toward retirement, they found themselves having to deal with health issues such as knee replacements, cardiac bypass, and cataract surgeries. To make matters worse, in her last year of running the business, Gladys came down with shingles due to the stress of life. Under the circumstances, there was no way that Bill and Gladys could realize their dream of retiring with sufficient resources to be comfortable. They had to keep working, despite continuing to lose money in the dance business and needing to borrow money from Susie.

After loaning them upwards of $40,000, Susie knew something had to be done. Not knowing how to get out of the situation, she and her parents turned to me for help. Since I own more than one business, I was immersed in the business world and had a plethora of resources available for Susie and her parents. I recommended that Bill and Gladys seek legal advice to deal with the credit card debt and remortgaging their property. After all, they had a large amount of equity in the property and it would allow Gladys and Bill to pay off the credit card companies and their daughter, and to pay back their debt at a much lower interest rate.

Unfortunately, the timing was not ideal as this was after the real estate crash and their financial situation was such that neither the banks nor the nontraditional business lenders believed they could pay back the loan. Gladys and Bill were just not fundable. Susie continued to loan them money that now exceeded $75,000 and was concerned that she was funding a bottomless pit.

The situation became even more urgent for Susie when her husband was laid off from his job. They had three children to support and their income went to zero. Fortunately, they had some savings and owned some rental properties. I recommended a financial advisor who helped leverage their money and assets to bring in more monthly income from high-yield investments while they re-established themselves. I recommended Susie use the money they had lent her parents as a down payment for purchasing the dance business and property.

By getting a mortgage on the property and buying the business, Susie got her loaned money back and, with her and her sisters' dance experience, they took over running the business with new energy and ideas. The business started to flourish and make money. With the help of the financial advisor I recommended, Susie used the money from their investments to help Bill and Gladys have money for retirement.

It was because of this experience that I became passionate about helping business owners get the money to continue running and expanding their businesses. I researched how business owners get money and where they go when banks won't lend. Along the way, I met my business partner, Chris Yurko, and together we formed C and C Funding. We have become the go-to people for options available for people who can't get lending from banks. We represent brokers and lending institutions outside of the banks. We can get nontraditional business loans or introduce business owners to a broker with access to banks and hard money lenders. We also have access to programs for business owners, dentists, and doctors to help their clients and patients find money as well.

Think about how many times a business owner, dentist, or doctor has heard someone say, "I would love to do that, but I just don't have the money," or "I know it would be worthwhile having that procedure done, but I don't have any health insurance."

We can help business owners reply with, "I have a lot of customers who run into that problem, and I now have a financing option available. Would you like to know more about it?"

What has been the hardest part of doing what you do?

The hardest part is meeting people who are not fundable who I can't help. So many people are finding themselves in desperate circumstances like Gladys and Bill. Or, they have the most amazing business idea, and even have their business established, but can't make it successful because they don't have enough money to invest in their own business, and they're not far enough along to be fundable. In this economy, start-up capital is pretty much non-existent unless someone can find a private investor.

Then there are people who come from profitable companies and the companies are suddenly shut down. Those people were not planning to go into their own businesses, but they see an opportunity to capitalize on their business relationships and continue servicing customers. They start their own businesses, re-establish contracts with the customers and business continues as usual. Because they, technically, have been in business for less than a year, they are not able to get a revolving line of business credit or any other business loan. These businesses are put in the start-up capital category by the lenders.

Then there are small, and very successful, businesses that banks just won't fund. Those people I can sometimes help.

What keeps you going when things are tough?

Every time I find a new situation, I do more research to find nontraditional lenders and sometimes I can help people. I'm very excited about this new product that can help business owners, dentists, and doctors help clients and patients get money when they need it most. The best thing is that this lending is not based on the borrower's credit score.

What's been the most rewarding part of what you do?

The most rewarding part of what I do is finding money for business owners and seeing the look of relief on their faces.

What is the most inspiring transformation or manifestation that you've witnessed in your work?

There are novel mechanisms that exist where people can get money; they just don't know about them. For example, I was referred to a beautiful, smart, and successful businesswoman. She owned a clothing store in Michigan and had a full-time job, as well as a high credit score. She wanted to establish a $7,000 revolving line of business credit. In the world of revolving credit, this is a very small amount. The bank would not fund her. Chris and I helped her find the money she needed to buy inventory for her store and she was very thankful for that. She pays back the money and then reapplies when she needs more. By using a nontraditional lender, she has created her own revolving line of credit. When I can help someone in this way, it inspires me to continue my business.

Marilyn Strong

"It takes a village to raise a child, but it takes a business to create a village. We need more businesses—and we need more villages."

During her early years as an ADD-diagnosed small business owner, Marilyn Strong often didn't feel very…well…strong. She just couldn't focus on what mattered every day. On the brink of bankruptcy, she started duct-taping whatever strategies did work into go-to daily routines.

That's when it happened.

As Marilyn engineered her routines to reliably skyrocket her own results, a few other entrepreneurs, who were also wrestling with ADD/ADHD symptoms, got curious. A few soon grew into dozens, and then Marilyn had to write a book, *Getting Paid to Pay Attention*, to help everyone asking for help—and the nearly 10 million adults, in North America alone, suffering from ADD/ADHD.

With 29 years of business experience in hand, Marilyn can help you cut through the ADD/ADHD fog to your own success.

In Marilyn's personal time, she's trekked all over Europe, many US states, Mexico, and her native British Columbia. She even once jumped in the Arctic Ocean for a "refreshing swim" and stayed up for 24 hours straight to enjoy the non-stop solstice daylight on the millennium's longest day (June 21, 2001) in Nunavut, Canada.

Marilyn holds an Executive MBA from Athabasca University in Information Technology Management, and she currently lives in the Okanagan region of British Columbia with musician Scott Pembleton.

To find out more: www.StrongBiz.com & marilyn@strongbiz.com

What personal event or universal problem made you want to do what you do?

The difficulties faced by adults with ADD and ADHD who are small business owners is more than a personal event for me, it's a universal problem. My generation was not tested for things like ADD or ADHD. All the teachers knew was that we couldn't sit still, couldn't focus, and were chatterers or were constant movers. We weren't paying attention because we *couldn't* pay attention; our brains wouldn't let us. We had to learn strategies to deal with it, so most of us didn't do well in school. For those who actually made it through, we were grateful we made it.

There are several parts to the problem facing those of us with ADD/ADHD. There's the issue of trying to find work that isn't boring (because we can be easily bored) that also doesn't put so much pressure on us that we end up feeling scattered and resort to extreme multi-tasking. To compensate for that pressure, we end up hyper-focusing and fueling ourselves on adrenaline and caffeine, and then, when that project or task is done, we collapse, exhausted. I went through that pattern for most of my career. After having had only three real "jobs" in my life, I discovered that I work much better for myself than others, but those ADD and ADHD characteristics continued to haunt me in my own business. I'd come up with a really cool idea for a project, get it all organized and ready, but then I wouldn't want to do it because I'd already done all the fun stuff, which was think about it, set it up, and get it organized. I wanted to go on to another project. So, when you're only focusing on the fun stuff, you forget to pay attention to really important things in your business—like the "business of the business."

Another universal problem, faced by adults with ADD/ADHD who have not been diagnosed, is that they're reluctant to get a diagnosis or even investigate what's going on with themselves. Adults with ADD or

ADHD are three times more likely to start a business than those without it. So, if you don't have ADD or ADHD, you *might* start a business, but if you *do* have it, you're three times more likely to start one. I've delivered trainings to thousands of people and many small businesses. I realized that this is a huge problem. These entrepreneurs and small business owners have *great* ideas, are incredibly creative, have value to add, and have messages to get out, but they can't keep their business going. I thought about what I did to help myself and I talked to some people, and they agreed. So, I sat down, did more research, and put the whole thing into a book.

The universal problem is that those with ADD and ADHD—whether they are diagnosed or not, or are in denial that they have it—are struggling in their businesses. They are barely keeping their heads above water. The world is based on small businesses and if we can't keep our small businesses going, we can't keep our families fed, we can't keep our communities healthy, and we can't keep our economy going. I feel it's my responsibility to help these small business owners focus on what they do best and help them create strategies so they can keep their businesses going without losing their energy, or their ambition and enthusiasm for what they do. There's nothing worse than a highly creative person being forced to sit down and do data entry for bookkeeping. That's just a waste of time and money. Over the years, that's what I've observed.

In 2007, I did a presentation at a Women in Business meeting. I was told that I could talk about any business topic, but I couldn't talk about what I did for a living. I procrastinated for weeks until the Sunday before the Wednesday presentation. I knew I had to get my presentation done. I wrote about trying to put together a presentation with my procrastination, my distractions, and my ADD. I told them the story about how I tried to pull this together and how I *succeeded*. Some of the things I talked about were funny—I got some laughs—and the audience came away with three strategies they could use any time they happened to procrastinate or got distracted. I had people coming up to me, afterward, telling me it was a fabulous presentation and I knew, then, that I had a winner. I knew, then, that what I'd been seeing, sensing, and feeling was *business* Attention Deficit Disorder. Businesses are being neglected. That was my "aha" moment.

What has been the hardest part of doing what you do?

There are two things. The first is getting past the stigma of ADD/ADHD, whether it's about admitting I have it or getting my clients to admit they have it. I was terrified to admit it myself. When my book came out, I thought, *okay, here it goes*, because there is a stigma attached to it and I am not the only one who recognizes that stigma. Trying to get others, who have it, to acknowledge it is really tough. That's okay because I didn't want to acknowledge it either. I knew it was in my family, and I knew I had it and it affected me, but I didn't want to think it controlled me. I figured: *I'm the only one who can control me.* When I talked to people about it and admitted I had it, I'd get a variety of reactions, from "Oh, God, I'd never hire you to do anything for me; you'd never get the job done," to "I'm so glad, because I think I have it, too. I'm having trouble with this. How can you help me?"

The second thing is focusing and remembering to apply my own strategies to my business when I'm working with other people. I have to use my own strategies to keep myself together because I could easily book my whole day working with other people and not invest time in managing my own business.

What keeps you going when things are tough?

Firstly, my mentors keep me going. I love and respect them, and I know that they love and respect me. I wouldn't do anything to disappoint them or myself. Whenever I get into one of my spins, I think: *What would so-and-so tell me? What would they suggest? Come on, Marilyn! Where's the coaching you've had all your life?*

The second thing is the unconditional love I have from my family and friends. They don't judge me; they just love me. My mentors, my family and friends, my clients—my *people*—that's what keeps me going…any person who sends me an email and says, "I want to learn more; how can you help me?" and I think: *Yes!*

What's been the most rewarding part of what you do?

The most rewarding part is talking with people and seeing the light come on in their eyes when I'm describing strategies for dealing with procrastination, distraction, and hyper-focus. Seeing the heads nod, seeing the notes being taken down, and seeing that my message is being absorbed and reflected back to me—that energy is so rewarding. The other thing that's really rewarding for me is the mentoring I'm doing. I'm helping people create rituals. I'm helping them learn to control the parts of their business they want to control and to delegate the rest. I'm helping them, more than coaching or anything else, as a mentor because I've had such fabulous mentors in my career. I'm helping people create whatever they need to be successful in their businesses. It takes a village to raise a child, but it takes a business to create a village. We need more businesses—and we need more villages.

What is the most inspiring transformation or manifestation that you've witnessed in your work?

In my book, I have two major strategies to organizing your day called the Little Picture and the Big Picture. Take a look at your Big Picture. How much time do you need between the time you wake up and when you sit at your desk, or stand in front of your X-ray machine, or greet clients at the door? Let's say you add a dog to your life. All of a sudden, you have to add another 30 minutes for a walk. How do you add that? How do you figure out lunches? How do you set that all up, so that you have everything ready and can focus on work? When people start to figure out that everything they're trying to cram into the morning means they need to get up at 4:00 or 4:30, rather than 5:30, 6:00, or 6:30, they start to understand why they're so frantic or late—because they're trying to cram so much in—another characteristic of having ADD and ADHD.

I really enjoyed watching the transformation of one particular client after he read my book. Once he got the Big Picture rituals straightened out in his mind and on paper, and got them working, he was a changed business owner. As soon as he started saying, "I can't take the dog for a walk. That's not my responsibility; it is your responsibility, kids, and that's the way it's going to be," he built in another half hour for himself. That meant that instead of taking the dog for a walk no matter what the weather was, he actually had 15 minutes for mindfulness and meditation. He could go into the master bathroom, calmly lock the door, and somebody else would take the dog for a walk. When he realized how much confusion and chaos there was in his morning, and he scrutinized all the time each activity took, the light bulb went on. More people in his family took responsibility for things that had been dumped on him, and he was off to the races. Next, he applied the same process to the details of his work projects and tasks, which set up his morning for success. He then applied to same process to his evening so that he was successful the next day. That was a huge transformation. Teaching that to one person, and watching him teach it to his family, was exciting.

Andrew Zirkin

"The mindset is what keeps me going—keeping a positive
mental attitude and keeping focused on my passions."

Andrew Zirkin is founder and CEO of a thriving Search Engine Optimization (SEO) company www.BrandSEO.com. He is also known as the World's First Expert in how SEO and Social Media Marketing work together. Andrew has been called "The King of SEO" by Chris Howard (World Leader in NLP) and has a client list that includes Mari Smith ("The Pied Piper of Facebook"), John Assaraf (*The Secret*), Jim Rohn (grandfather of Personal Development), Ben Gay III (author of *The Closers*) and Ram Das (author of *Be Here Now*).

Andrew has been featured on the TV show, "House Hunters International" and interviewed by TV Host Letitia Wright of "The Wright Place," Christopher Howard, and Clinton Swaine of www.FrontierTrainings. com. He has spoken at events hosted by Mari Smith, Chris Howard, Mensa Regional 2010, HISCEC Business Showcase, Tiscali Events London, and BNI weekly events. Andrew is a collaborative author on *The Power of Mentorship Series* and is also an author of several articles and press releases on the subjects of SEO 2.0 and social media, and how to increase business through effective Internet marketing.

To find out more: www.WealthMagnets.com &
andrew@brandseo.com

What personal event or universal problem made you want to do what you do?

The short answer to this question is that I was looking for a perfect form of marketing—a low-cost, very effective form of marketing—and I was looking for assets to gain financial freedom that didn't require me to be in one location or one city, something that I could keep building even if I moved from one place to another. At the moment, I live in Thailand, so I was able to take what I did in San Diego and move it to Thailand very easily.

I've been in some form of business or another ever since I was in the seventh grade, when I used to sell gummy bears. Throughout my life I've been a businessperson, and I've always had some sort of business, or sold something, on the side. I didn't have some sort of big transformation like someone who works in a corporation, let's say, and one day the sky falls, and all of a sudden they start an online business—or some sort of business—and shift from one thing to another. There are a couple of pivotal shifts I talk about in my website I'm working on right now, www. AndrewZirkin.com. I had a screen-printing business in my 20s for eight years. I did a Learning Annex class in guerilla marketing with J. Conrad Levinson and, even though I'd had my screen-printing business, I didn't understand that the shirts I was printing were guerilla marketing! Shirts were a low-cost, very effective form of marketing that small businesses could use; they could make money by selling the shirts that promoted their coffee shop, band, or whatever it was. It was almost a paid form of getting their marketing out there. It was definitely a form of guerilla marketing because people walk around and wear the shirts for years! Even if people gave them away for free, it promoted the companies and built the brands. Understanding that in that one-day class with J. Conrad Levinson was a big shift for me. He wasn't super-famous at the time; I wish I had stayed connected with him because he *did* get super-famous with his brand and his books!

The next shift happened after I went to art school at UC Santa Cruz. I studied in Rome, I traveled through Europe, and I had a great life in my 20s. It was very relaxed; I wasn't rich, but I was doing what I wanted to do, studying healing arts, martial arts, and fine arts, the latter that I got my degree in. After I graduated from school, I wondered, "What's the next act? What do I do?" My degree in fine art was not a very money-making, marketable skill; it can be, but it's difficult. I was living in London at the time somebody handed me the book, *Rich Dad, Poor Dad*. It's quite a simple book, but the concept of building assets that would bring money into my life, as opposed to working hard, was new. Even in my screen-printing business, I had to work hours in trade for money; there wasn't the leverage of recurring income. Customers would come back six months later because we'd have their screens, and I'd get in the shop and print more shirts for them, but it didn't have much leverage. I had the same problem every time I moved. When I moved from Los Angeles to Santa Cruz for art school, a lot of the stuff I did in LA, like the screen-printing, didn't work any more. Santa Cruz was a small town—there weren't a lot of businesses to sell to—so I had to reinvent myself and figure out the answer to the universal challenge of, "How do we make money?" As long as we're running a system of money in our world, we have to have money ourselves, or have someone else covering us. Even Gandhi and Mother Theresa had access to money. When they wanted a school built, someone else came, put the money up, and the school was built. They may not have personally had a lot of money, but they were able to control money.

So, when I moved to Santa Cruz, I had to change my ways, just as I had to when moving to London, but now I had that information about building assets. I got involved with network marketing in London. I built a team of 200 people in a great company that paid great compensation and great bonuses. It was a really good network marketing opportunity and was a very easy one to sell. When I showed it to people, most of them about fifty to sixty percent of the people who looked at it—would join. My business grew pretty fast and I made good money at it. Within the first month, I made a full time income, and after a year, it got better. I also started sourcing real estate for people in London. I studied the real estate market there and I got paid to source real estate, so I studied real estate investing, and I also got involved with a friend of mine in Internet marketing. This was back in 2002 to 2003, pretty early still, and I was excited about it. I liked the idea of Internet marketing because it was something I could move from place to place. Unfortunately, the network marketing company I had built up was only based in Europe. At the time, I had planned to stay in London and Europe, so there was no challenge with that, but then my mom got very sick back in Los Angeles. I had told myself I would never move back to LA, since I had lived there over 25 years, but I decided it was more important to be with my mom than to stay in London and build this networking company.

When I moved from London back to Los Angeles, the same challenge came up again, of how to start making money in LA. I polished up my resume (I actually had six versions of it because I had so many different skills) and went after several different types of jobs. I really wanted to do something in Internet marketing. I was hired by a Search Engine Optimization (SEO) company to get websites to the top of search engines that's where I learned about that skill. I really wanted to learn it anyway for my own projects! I worked for them for about a year, but I saw where they had mistreated their clients, in terms of the work they did, their ethics, and some other issues. For about a year, I did some consulting and some bigger SEO projects. Then I decided to start www. BrandSEO.com as the perfect way to market with low-cost, effective techniques guerilla marketing. Search Engine Optimization (getting websites to the top of search engines)was the perfect model for me because people go to search engines to look for these services and products anyway! I built up BrandSEO to provide that service for my customers. I built it up to around $150,000 a year in revenue at its peak, and it's been an incredible journey. I've been doing Search Engine Optimization for about seven years, so I'm one of the earlier pioneer-innovators in the industry. In the last year or two, I've shifted over to an education model;

I'm working on creating products to teach people how to better their marketing, since I'm versed in so many types of marketing. I really love working with, coaching, and consulting people, and I'm building some mastermind groups and programs.

What has been the hardest part of doing what you do?

The hardest part is also one of the most fun and best parts—it's really the fact that what I do changes almost daily! I'm always learning new things, which I *love* to do—that's my style, that's who I am and it's what I love. But sometimes, it can be a little taxing on the brain. Learning new skill sets can be difficult, but as a business owner in current, modern times, you have to learn how to do that.

What keeps you going when things are tough?

I've done a lot of personal development work so, when times do get tough, I have to revert back to the mindset work that I've done and remind myself that life's a roller coaster. It goes up, it goes down. We choose how we feel and think on a daily basis. I can choose to be unhappy or upset. Everyone in the world, as far as I know, gets angry, upset, and has ups and downs, but when I get angry or upset, the key is shifting that as quickly as possible—not staying angry. It used to be five minutes, now I try to make it five seconds; I just don't stay in a negative space. The mindset is what keeps me going—keeping a positive mental attitude and keeping focused on my passions.

What's been the most rewarding part of what you do?

Part of it is meeting great people! I've built a huge international network not just in San Diego, but throughout the world—of amazing people whom I talk to and work with, and who support me. The community that we have, throughout the planet, of conscious entrepreneurs, of the human potential movement, keeps me in a really cool space—the marketers, personal development people, and the human beings I meet that make a difference. I think that a lot of people in our community are living much closer to their human potential than the average person out there.

What is the most inspiring transformation or manifestation that you've witnessed in your work?

It's funny, because when we're doing testimonials, we're always looking for a financial story. For example, we had a client who sold an extra 25 million dollars in real estate, in a down market, from our Search Engine Optimization work. That's *incredible*—25 million extra in real estate sales, just from the SEO that we did for him! Money is energy; I like the word "currency" because it's current. I know that money doesn't buy happiness, as they say (and many other expressions), but not having it definitely makes people unhappy, and it makes life a challenge if they can't pay the bills. Because I focus on marketing and business, I've helped shift people's incomes and revenues drastically through the work that I've done. It's rewarding to see how my mentoring and coaching have helped people create shifts in their lives and lifestyles, so they're much happier on a daily basis, in many more areas of their lives than just the financial.

Spiritual Development

Emile Gauvreau

"I see myself as a teacher, a counselor, and an example of what others can do when they explore and allow themselves to realize the truth within them."

Rev. Emile Gauvreau began his service with the Center for Spiritual Living Cape Coral in June 2008. His intention is to build upon the legacy of the Center's founders, who planted its roots over 40 years ago. Rev. Emile is dedicated to the personal and spiritual transformation of each individual touched by the Center for Spiritual Living. He knows that the Science of Mind philosophy—coupled with the universal truths of New Thought-Ancient Wisdom—is a vehicle to open hearts to their true calling. Rev. Emile's intention is to be part of a dynamic, growing spiritual community that realizes the benefits of these teachings. His vision is for the Center for Spiritual Living Cape Coral, and its members, to be a beneficial presence in the world.

Rev. Gauvreau is a graduate of the University of Transformation and Spiritual Leadership at the Agape International Spiritual Center in Los Angeles, California. While at Agape International Spiritual Center, he served in many capacities including over six years as a member of the Board of Trustees, and the Consciousness of Wealth Committee. He has served as an active Agape Licensed Practitioner for almost a decade. He also served as the Youth and Family Director for the Claremont Church of Religious Science in Claremont, California. He currently serves as the Vice President of the Board of Trustees of the Science of Mind Foundation.

Join Emile at Center for Spiritual Living Cape Coral in the celebration of the expression of the divine as it demonstrates itself in the world as you.

To find our more: www.CenterForSpiritualLivingCC.com & (239) 574-6463

What personal event or universal problem made you want to do what you do?

I'm not sure that anything *made* me do what I do, or made me *want* to do it; it was sort of an inevitable path. I was probably six, at the earliest point, when I was sent to catechism class at a local Catholic church. The information was fine. I was memorizing and all that good stuff but I felt, at the time, that the nuns appeared to be very spiritual beings and that they knew something they weren't telling the rest of us. They knew something beyond the pages of the book and the words they asked us to memorize and the ideas that were going on. That turned on a switch, within me, that said: *I need to know more about these things they're calling "God" and "religion."* And that put me on a path that continued over the next, literally, 40 years through various activities.

The next major event was seeing the first *Star Wars* movie. In "The Force," I got that there was something out there, something I could be in harmony and balance with, and allow to work through me. I just kept remembering Luke Skywalker's words: "Let the Force be with you. Let it be with you. Let it be with you." So when I discovered Science of Mind in 1996, it was like: *Oh! Somebody's actually organized this thing. Somebody's actually talking more about it.* Then the questions really started to come and I had no choice, really. It was a matter of learning more, studying more, expanding more, and when I saw a position open and I wasn't even looking for it, saying to myself: *This church needs a minister.* I needed to apply. I needed to step up into the role that I have now, in which I consider myself a spiritual mentor. I don't pretend to direct or, necessarily, lead; I see myself as a teacher, a counselor, and an example of what others can do when they explore and allow themselves to realize the truth within them.

What has been the hardest part of doing what you do?

The hardest part has been having balance to do my own spiritual work. One of the beauties of what I do is, in effect, my biggest responsibility. To keep myself spiritually tuned and attuned sometimes causes me to be less tuned to the actual physical, material world. So, it's a constant effort to maintain that balance, and bring myself back into balance so that I, number one, take care of my own physical being, make sure that I'm healthy, and all those things so I can do my work. Also, from the material world aspect, to prepare the things that come along with having a church, like the building, people, parking spaces, air conditioning, and being aware that, *oh, there's a hurricane coming, maybe we should put up the hurricane shutters,"* rather than thinking, *oh, we're all right because we're in a God bubble and everything is fine.* It's balancing those things and having techniques to focus on the physical world things I need to do as I'm doing my spiritual work.

What keeps you going when things are tough?

I have the underlying thought (I don't know when I ever didn't have it) that no matter what is going on, I will be okay. So, when stuff happens, after I have my initial reaction, I have the thought that everything will be okay. I don't know what "okay" will look like, and it's usually not the same as things were before. I think it started when I was a small child. I'd hear about world events and major things happening, and the next day I still had to get up and go to school, and do whatever I needed to do, and go to bed the next night—brush my teeth and all that stuff—and I was okay. I didn't have any concept of what might have been happening in the world, but at the same time, stuff was happening and I was okay. And that's been more solidified for me as I've done more of my spiritual growth and development. I understand that whatever happened is over, and I'm still here. Now, what is there to learn and do about the conditions that exist around me?

What's been the most rewarding part of what you do?

The most rewarding part is "seeing the light go on" in people in class, or on a Sunday morning, or in a conversation over a cup of coffee; their whole demeanor changes.

"Oh my goodness, that's what's been going on? Now I see what I need to do, where I need to go!"

Two weeks ago, a woman was so excited to tell me that she had this major revelation that changed her life from being depressed and unemployed to having a job offer and starting a new job within the course of four days!

She said, "It was something you said."

I never know what it was I said that hit somebody, but it's something they heard in a different way than they've ever heard it before, or they've heard it enough times and finally, the fourth or the seventeenth time, or the twenty-seventh time they hear it—and it happens to be from me—it pushes them over the edge to, "Oh my goodness!"

To see people changing their lives, getting healthy, getting jobs, starting businesses...it's an exciting energy when people are fully engaged in what they're doing. It's very exciting to be blessed with seeing it.

What is the most inspiring transformation or manifestation that you've witnessed in your work?

The one that comes forward is actually one I experienced myself, because it demonstrated that what I was thinking and feeling was somehow in the right energetic. I had been working for a large medical group for about five years, as a consultant, which had provided me with a very nice income over that period of time. I worked with them and they merged with two other medical groups, and then needed to hire a CEO. They held interviews and I actually had my interview late on a Wednesday evening, and the very next morning got on a plane with my then-19-year-old son and went to Europe for three and a half weeks.

While I was in Europe, I called home and spoke with the finance officer of the organization, who worked for me. He told me that I had not been selected for the position, that they hired somebody else. I had a reaction—disappointment and so on—and that evening, when I was on a train from Paris to Amsterdam, I started making a list. On the list were about 20 people I needed to call, when I got back to the United States, to line up my next work. At that point, it was early September and my group work with this medical group would be done by the end of December.

When I got home, I became immediately involved in the final activities of merging these medical groups and shutting down the one I had been running. I was running about a 50-million-dollar company, and the merger created about a 75-million-dollar company. While I was doing all this work, I didn't have a chance to pick up the phone to call any of the people on my list, but by the end of November, all of them had called me, and by the middle of December, I had replaced the income I would be losing from this group and actually increased it by about 50 percent for the next year.

What I had relaxed into was that thing I talked about earlier—knowing I was okay. Something obviously didn't go the way I had wanted it to, but I knew I was okay. Then, like in *Star Wars*, I leaned into the knowing that there was this Force that surrounded me and moved with me. It would be about two and a half years before I actually discovered the Science of Mind teaching that would basically give me words and structures to understand what had happened, but I got the sense that there was something very strong out there and it *was* for me. It was *not* against me, and if I allowed it to work for me, I would be able to use it and teach it, and have others be inspired by it.

So, as I do my work, I really feel that I'm obligated to simply share and find that space that opens the door of realization for whoever it is I'm speaking with. It's been almost 20 years since that very transformative period in my life put me on the track that contributed to what I am today.

Wendy J. Vitalich

"It's inspiring witnessing couples finding their way back to love again, and seeing teenagers when they're able to share with me the courage they had when they put their courage suit on and were able to speak up."

Wendy J. Vitalich is a Marriage and Family Therapy (MFT) Intern supervised by Rebecca Kahane, a licensed MFT, who maintains a private practice in El Segundo, California. She will be taking the licensing exam by early 2013.

Wendy earned a BA Degree in Psychology from Ramapo College in Mahwah, New Jersey, and an MA Degree in Clinical Psychology from Antioch University in Culver City, California.

She specializes in individuals, couples, families, parenting issues, divorce, loss of a loved one, adolescent issues, preteens, and teens. Wendy offers self-esteem building along with coaching her clients to become aware and shift out of old, stuck patterns. Her goal is to assist clients in achieving emotional balance in the face of life's daily challenges.

Wendy is a single mother of a teenage daughter. Her job placement business, for the past 21 years, has become part-time as she maintains a full-time therapy practice. She is the author of a new book, *Unspoken Agreements: A Twin's Journey and Beyond*, and a member of the Agape International Spiritual Center, where she has sung with the Agape International Choir for the past eight years.

To find out more: www.WendyJVitalich.com & wvitalich@gmail.com & (310) 344-8182

What personal event or universal problem made you want to do what you do?

My childhood traumas were my personal event. I did not have anyone to talk to when I was dealing with an alcoholic father and a mother who was too afraid to protect. There was a lot of fear that I took on and that controlled a lot of my life. I see that issue a lot with kids when they don't have a voice or they feel like they can't speak up—and, actually, this happens with adults, too. I wanted to give back. I finally got support when I became an adult and I really saw how talking it out and being able to have a safe place really helped me.

The universal problem is that many people don't know how to communicate, let alone have the courage they need to speak up. I work with a lot of different people in my therapy practice but I have a special soft spot for children who are going through the divorce situation with their parents. A line that I came up with over 30 years ago is, "Children of divorce don't have a choice, but they do have a voice." I offer that safety for them to speak and find their voices.

What has been the hardest part of doing what you do?

Personally, the hardest part is judging the time schedule. I love what I do so it's not difficult. The other part that's challenging is that I'm an intern—I have about 400 hours (or less) to go. I want to be able to help many, many people so I'm a little limited with my schedule and I pack people in when I can. For me, the hardest part is juggling that while I run my other business and raise my teenager as I'm a single mom.

What keeps you going when things are tough?

What keeps me going, regarding my therapy practice, is that this has been a 30-year dream for me. Holding onto my vision of how I can make a difference to the individuals, couples, families, children, and teenagers who come into my office keeps me going when things are tough, and when I have a schedule that's nuts and I'm running all over the place. When I'm in my office, there's a difference that's made, a positive effect, whether it's a tool that they've learned, that they feel safe, that I get them, that they feel like they have someone they can lean on or talk to. That makes it all worth it, when I can be of service in the healing process.

What's been the most rewarding part of what you do?

The most rewarding part is being a witness to someone's awareness when they wake up...when they have their "aha" moments...when they are able to navigate their way to find more joy in their life. Whether it be to change some old patterns and old ways of thinking or having the courage to speak up or stand up to someone that they've needed to, it's very rewarding when I get feedback from my clients that they are happier and are living a more joyful life within their work, in their personal lives, and in their relationships. When I can help parents with parenting skills, that's very rewarding.

What is the most inspiring transformation or manifestation that you've witnessed in your work?

It's inspiring witnessing couples finding their way back to love again, and seeing teenagers when they're able to share with me the courage they had when they put their courage suit on and were able to speak up. Perhaps their motto had been, "Why bother? It won't matter anyway," and then they realize that it *does* matter and *they* matter.

As far as the most inspiring transformation, I have many stories in my practice. I'm working with many couples who were on the brink of divorce and I watch them go, through their commitment and their willingness, from being ready to file the papers to, "We have this amazing connection again!" They have communication skills that they didn't have before. They are listening to each other differently, validating each other, empathizing, and really opening their hearts to each other.

I think that the other wonderful transformation is with my teens. It is wonderful when a teen calls me directly and says, "I want to come in and make an appointment because I need to talk." The courage I see is inspiring. I have a couple of teenagers who have really built their backbone and that's really wonderful. That's their doing. I'm just shining a light for them to walk down a certain path.

Jess Steinman

*"I have come to believe—and not just to believe, but to know—
that each of us has the power within us to a) heal, and
b) manifest whatever it is that we desire."*

Jess Steinman is an intuitive tarot reader and teacher, psychic medium, Integrated Energy Therapy® Master Instructor, Advanced Reiki Practitioner, and practitioner of Crystal Healing and Total Energetics: The Science & Art of Trance-Formation. Originally a skeptic of this work herself, Jess spent her early years, and into college, studying both instrumental and vocal music. After having what Jess terms as her "quarter life crisis" in 2002, she was introduced to psychics, mediums, and spiritual and energy healing and, as she jokingly says now, "I'm never going back!"

Jess has had the opportunity to work for nationally-known psychic medium and author, Suzane Northrop, as well as participate in workshops and seminars with two other nationally-known psychic mediums and authors, John Holland and Patti Sinclair.

From experiencing readings by many different psychics, intuitives, and mediums, Jess has come to believe that readings can be a loving, healing experience, often leading to growth and acceptance of our true selves and our situations. If you've never been read before, having a reading (or an energy healing session) with Jess is a wonderful opportunity and a very safe place to start. If it has been a while since your last reading or energy healing session, Jess invites you to join her and reconnect with your spirit. You will find that whether it is a reading, class, or hands-on energy work, Jess has a passion for assisting others in their self-healing process and enjoys teaching them how to self-heal through mediumship, tarot, Integrated Energy Therapy®, Reiki, Crystal Healing and Total Energetics.

To find out more: www.InTouchWithSpirit.com

What personal event or universal problem made you want to do what you do?

It was during what I call my "quarter life crisis." I was 22 years old, and I had just left college on a medical leave, halfway through pursuing a six-year music education program. I came home and my world was turned upside down. I was no longer a student, I wasn't a regular practicing musician, and on top of it, my paternal grandmother had passed away. All of this sent my world into a tailspin for a good year to year and a half, trying to figure out where I was going, what my next steps were, and who I was. I didn't believe in any of this spiritual work that I now do. I thought that all people who do what I do—all psychics…all mediums— were frauds. I was in a very "down" space.

It took going to a seminar by a well-known psychic medium, and having a meditation where my grandmother came through clear as day, to get me out of that space. It totally blew me away! Suddenly, my fear of death— which had been with me as a child, through my teenage years, and into my twenties—was no longer there. I began questioning *everything* I had thought. As I did this, I started reading voraciously and taking classes to try to understand all that had suddenly happened to me. As I was taking these classes (energy-healing classes and classes for spiritual and psychic development) I started to do private sessions and readings for friends on the side, thinking I would return to music eventually.

As I did more sessions for other people, they started to say to me, "Jess, you're really good at this! You should do this."

I resisted and resisted. Finally, what happened is that Spirit, as it often does, created a bunch of synchronicities that opened doors for me and allowed me to step into doing this as a business. It was something I had never imagined. I often joke about being a medium and say that I never thought I'd be "caught dead" doing the work that I do. Spirit just worked it out, and here I am, doing this work that I absolutely love. But it was because of that questioning, and that "quarter life crisis," that I got started.

What has been the hardest part of doing what you do?

The hardest part is dealing with skepticism—not so much from other people, because I understand coming from that place of being a skeptic, but instead dealing with my own skepticism or my own self-doubt. There are still moments when I go into that human space, that ego- or fear-based space, and I say to myself: *Is this real? Is this working? Am I even supposed to do this, really?* It's getting past that negative self-talk that still shows up from time to time. I notice that when I go through it, I also have clients who come to me and mirror those thoughts for me. That's a challenging piece, but I'm learning from it each time I walk through it.

What keeps you going when things are tough?

There are three things that keep me going. The first is my support system of friends and mentors around me. I've created an incredible web of support that really lifts me up when things are down.

The second piece is remembering how far I've come…taking a look back, thinking back to when I was 22 and 23 and searching for things, and seeing how far that journey has brought me.

The last piece is thinking about my clients. I deal with a lot of clients who are going through really challenging situations. I think about the very deep grief they are working through—losses of children or long-time partners or best friends—and watch them getting up every day and putting one foot in front of the other. I say to myself: *If they can do it, so can I.*

What's been the most rewarding part of what you do?

The most rewarding part is watching my clients and my students when they have "that moment." My business name is In Touch with Spirit, and it's rewarding for me to watch that moment when I see my clients or students really are getting in touch with spirit, whether they feel the spirit or the energy of a loved one who has crossed over in the room with us, or perhaps they feel a deeper connection to their own Higher Self through meditating or through a session that I've done with them, or they're feeling a greater connection to God, to the Spirit of the Universe, that connects all of us. When I see that spark—that look in their eyes— that is the best feeling in the world.

What is the most inspiring transformation or manifestation that you've witnessed in your work?

Starting within myself, and now seeing it in clients, I have come to believe—and not just to believe, but to know—that each of us has the power within us to a) heal, and b) manifest whatever it is that we desire.

Last year, I moved into a new home. The first night in the new home, I was walking down the stairs, and actually bringing my cat down the stairs with me to familiarize her with the new house. At the second step from the top, my foot slipped out from under me and I took a ride down the entire stairwell. At the bottom of the stairs, I lay there, unsure whether I had broken, bruised, or sprained anything. As I tried to figure out what to do next—*Do I try to get up? Do I try to move? What happens next?*—I heard this little voice, within me, that said: *This is going to be your opportunity, your test, to see how much you believe in the ability to heal yourself from within.*

I slowly picked myself up and brought myself back up the stairs. I sat there for about an hour with an ice pack on my head and doing energy work on myself. I kept seeing myself healing swiftly and easily, and something that many people told me would take six to eight weeks to heal, because I was so badly bruised from head to toe (amazingly with no breaks or sprains), took me two-and-a-half to three weeks! There were no painkillers involved, no trips to hospitals or doctors or anything of the sort; it was just natural healing…a little bit of arnica, a little bit of energy work, and the rest was just visualizing.

I know that is a rare thing, and I've told clients this story and said to them, "I'm not telling you not to go to your doctor when you need it. I'm not telling you not to get things treated when they need to be treated." But I just *knew* deep inside of me that I had the power to heal this from within.

When I share that story with clients, friends, and students, it creates that light in their eyes.

They say, "Wow! You did it? I can do it, too!"

It's a great reminder for myself, also; when things get tough, I remember: *Yes, I was able to heal from that, so I can heal from this, too.*

Georgena Eggleston

"Celebrating the new beliefs people embody and embracing, with my clients, the gifts grief has for them keeps me going."

Georgena Eggleston earned her M.A. in Speech-Language Pathology from the University of Nebraska—Lincoln. After several decades of facilitating communication with people of all ages, she wanted to learn to listen differently and coach others to do the same. She became certified in the Rubenfeld Synergy Method® after her four year training with Ilana Rubenfeld, its founder. It was during this time that she moved through her own embodied grief to become a Master Grief Practitioner.

Georgena became certified in PSCH-K® and developed Affirmative Innergetics® with Carolyn Winkler in Portland, Oregon. She completed Clean Language and Symbolic Modeling, Clean Space and Emergent Knowledge Certifications with Marian Way from Hampshire England. As the "Loss Lady," Georgena sees clients in her Portland, Oregon office or facilitates sessions on the phone or via Skype.

Georgena is also the author of the soon to be released book, *A New Mourning: Embracing the Gifts in Grief.*

To find out more: www.JoyWithGeorgena.com

What personal event or universal problem made you want to do what you do?

Have you ever heard someone say, or felt like saying yourself, "I'm so embarrassed, I want to die"?

My fifteen-and-a-half-year old son, Reed—handsome, sensitive, gifted, mathematician, visual artist, athlete, and charismatic leader—felt that. When he was suspended for three days as a ninth grader and was banned from the basketball team for the rest of the year, his world came to an end. He had failed the breath test, and although his classmates had been drinking, too, he had been caught. He had failed publicly, and he lost face. While I was comforting his girlfriend, Reed—who had lettered in cross-country as a freshman—ran home. He leaned over the barrel of a shotgun, and died of impulse-icide. His journals had plans to letter in five sports during his high school career, clearly stated plans for a future with hope.

It was this grief that brought me to my knees, even though grief had been a companion for the previous three-and-a-half years. During that time, my brother, Mark, and parents, Betty and George, had all died. Grief gripped my body. I, the successful businesswoman, held myself even tighter that spring and summer. Courage and faith that I would move through the sobbing, the longing, and the fear kept me going, one foot in front of the other. My time in stillness increased, and I learned to listen with my eyes, hear with my heart, and see with my intuition.

So, I am the "Loss Lady." Divorce, loss of a home, loss of a business, death of a sibling, parents, and a child have all been my story.

What has been the hardest part of doing what you do?

Moving through the shame and guilt that I did not parent my child safely through adolescence has been the hardest, which led me to face my belief that I was unworthy and never enough. Knowing that the processes I was led to develop were more than enough for me, and others, to move from grief's grip to radiant joy allowed me to move through.

What keeps you going when things are tough?

Increasing relaxation, stillness, and the peace others and I experience and discover as we move through our loss keeps me going. Witnessing people dialoguing with their embodied grief keeps me going. Celebrating the new beliefs people embody and embracing, with my clients, the gifts grief has for them keeps me going.

What's been the most rewarding part of what you do?

I have several stories to share because it's amazing what happens in a very short amount of time.

In the first story, a woman said, "I want to like the mother of my daughter-in-law. Right now, she is always late, and it's driving me crazy!"

As we moved through the affirmative energetics process to create her new belief, she was able to shift her relationship with time itself. The mother-in-law wasn't the problem; it was my client's experience with time. As she relaxed into her new awareness, her tensions with the other woman vanished.

In the second story, a man said to me, "I really miss my former wife."

He had divorced her twice.

By teaching him a simple process in less than five minutes, he called the next day to say, "That really works! I already feel more loving toward myself. I *am* a good guy!"

Soon after that, he began to train for a half-marathon to celebrate his 65th birthday.

And in the third story, a woman was fired from her marketing job of many years. Even though she knew that economics were the bottom line that drove this decision, she still felt shame and resentment toward her boss. Fifteen minutes into a session of Clean Space, she forgave her boss and began laughing as she discovered the support and freedom of her current situation. She left my office empowered!

There are many stories that allow me to know that little rewards are here and there for other people. As they embody their grief, they discover the gifts of their grief and are able to release grief quickly these are all wonderful rewards for me.

What is the most inspiring transformation or manifestation that you've witnessed in your work?

The most inspiring story was a mom who had buried her 30-year-old son. Like my son, Reed, her son was also handsome, charismatic, and artistically gifted.

She found me online, came in and said, "I want to feel my heart again. I don't know who I am."

She was obviously hopeless. We discussed some possibilities for her and decided that she would benefit most from the 30-day grief program, in which she called every morning as soon as she got up, sometimes as early as 4:30 a.m. In these calls, she was able to release the grief and begin to listen to what she wanted that day to be. On the phone, she began discovering her embodied grief, so she ended up coming for three personal sessions over three months. In those three sessions, she was able to heal not only her heart, but really be in her body once again, and she was able to discover a meaningful direction for her life. When she walked out, she was truly in radiant joy. She inspires me to this day! Every time I think about her—because our sons were so similar—I'm incredibly grateful to have been her companion from grief's grip to radiant joy.

Romae Lenci

*"My passion is helping people know that love
is their main purpose on this Earth."*

Rev. Romae Lenci is an ordained minister, a life coach, and a spiritual counselor. She was ordained as a non-denominational minister through a metaphysical fellowship church in Anaheim, California in 1998.

Rev. Romae is currently officiating God's glorious connections at beautiful sandy beaches on the island of Kauai. She has done many weddings in California at all types of venues—homes, beaches, museums, hotels, and also in churches—and she's willing to travel to your location, if the need arises.

Her ceremonies can vary depending on the couple's background. She believes the couple should choose the right sayings and words to express their love for one another to create a bond in bliss and love. She will add a Hawaiian touch to whatever the couple's needs are.

Her background in fashion design and floral design help her guide her brides with their dress and their flowers too. She has also been involved as a life coach for 23 years, helping people love themselves by releasing weight spiritually. That is one of her many gifts for brides who want to do that for that important day.

She has been told, by many of her couples, that she brings magic to the ceremony.

To find out more: www.CAB1111.com & (808) 639-3787 &
revromae@cab1111.com

What personal event or universal problem made you want to do what you do?

When I was younger, I was this little girl that just loved everything about life. I was in nature, I was playing, I was happy all the time.

I actually said, one day, to my mom, "Mom, why aren't people nice to each other? People should love each other!"

She said to me, "Yes, that's the way it should be, but it doesn't always work that way."

I was little—I was probably about four—and she looked at me like: *Who are you?* I became very focused on being happy, positive about life, enjoying every minute, and having fun (not that there weren't any problems).

As I matured and decided that life was really about loving each other, I really took to heart, "Love one another as you love yourself." For me, it became my motto. My thought process, overall, was: *If I take care of me and I'm loved, then I can love anybody else in the world.* It became easier, and I really worked hard at that, because it's not always easy to put yourself first in this world.

After I became an ordained minister, I had attended a few weddings and something, inside of me, happened. I felt in a totally different space, even about love, and the passion was: *I want to connect people. I think that is something I was born to do.* As an ordained minister, I started doing weddings in 1998 and the next thing I knew, I was doing sermons and celebrations of life because I knew there was always a thread of love that went through those ceremonies.

I recently moved to Kauai, Hawaii, and I'm *very* passionate about facilitating God's glorious connections in this most beautiful, colorful place, doing weddings and renewals because not only is this a mystical place, but it's magical, with the most romantic settings in the world. My passion is helping people know that love is their main purpose on this Earth.

What has been the hardest part of doing what you do?

It's very, very interesting how this question comes up for me because a lot of times I'll see people who *say* they love each other, in a wedding situation, and I think they may not understand that they have to see each other as God-beings, not as just another person they're going to marry, and I'll take them back to, "You have to love yourself, too." I think one of the hardest parts is to make that really, really strong in setting up a relationship. Once we see that we're all connected, loving ourselves is easier than loving others just because we might get something back. I think it becomes really important to put love as a priority but, again, you have to love yourself first, in order to love anybody else. Once we get to that place of understanding that love is always there, and it's not about fear of walking into a bad situation, we can really love and heal each other, and care for the other person a lot more deeply.

A lot of people will get married and not stay married. It's hard for me because I saw the love at the beginning, and then I hear the couple is divorced. One of the things I say to couples is, "You guys aren't getting married just because it's going to make income tax better!" It's hard to see people separate because they lost that initial blissful feeling of being in love.

What keeps you going when things are tough?

My prayer and meditation discipline has become such a priority and habit for me that whenever I feel worried or distressed or troubled, I go back to center. I do this as a ritual, every single morning. I do spiritual readings, I pray, I do yoga, I mediate, and I have a mentor, Dr. Wayne Dyer. He taught me how to do an "Ah" chant that I've done for almost 16

years. In that chant, I let go of the outside world and open up my soul. I
see the most incredible colors and light in that place. Every time I go into
that mediation, I get guidance, relaxation, and a vibration that's much
higher than any worry I could ever have. I think it's God's guidance.
It keeps me strong in my faith and I really trust better when I feel that
centering. That's what I call "the love." That always moves me forward
instead of being stuck.

What's been the most rewarding part of what you do?

Again, going back to the feelings of love that surround any ceremony I
do. It's not just weddings or even celebrations of life. The love that comes
through when somebody passes on—makes their transition—I love that
feeling; I think it's magical! I don't know where it comes from but it's a
different feeling when you know love is present. One of the things that
I do, especially at weddings, is take the bride and groom aside and I do
a silent meditation with them. Basically, I vibrationally raise their hearts
to open. I know, for them, that they're not in fear and even if this whole
situation fell apart on them, they would be able to handle it with grace
and ease. They usually come out of the ceremony feeling confident in
their love, their commitment and realize that there truly is a love that
happens in this silent meditation we did together. I've had a few people,
after my ceremonies, walk up to me and say, "This was so different. I
don't know what you did, but it was so different!" That's the passion that
runs through me when I connect people. It lifts me up—and everybody
else, too. That's really exciting for me. That's been my authentic passion,
to connect people. It doesn't always have to be in a wedding; it can be in a
relationship or a work setting where people are not getting along, or just
staying centered, helping people understand who they are, and making
a difference.

What is the most inspiring transformation or manifestation that you've witnessed in your work?

I was asked to perform my very first wedding by a young woman who, through my job at Weight Watchers, I had helped manifest this absolutely self-centered love.

She had fallen in love with herself, and she walked up to me and said, "You have helped me transform my whole life. Will you perform my wedding?"

I did, and it was the most incredible ceremony and energy, not just with her, but the whole family, the photographer, the cake, everything! It was the most incredible feeling I've ever had.

I've watched this couple, Andy and Donna, grow together in all the bad and all the good. They now have four children and a family who supports them. They both have great jobs and a wonderful home. It's wonderful to see that first love connection—of the couple that rolled right into their family and the kids—and it stayed there.

Ten years later, they said, "You need to remarry us when we hit our ten year anniversary."

That love connection becomes a passion that stays with families. It has been very inspiring for me to know that it's not always a disappointment. It's been pretty fun to watch this couple! They built a relationship around their love for each other and their family. That really got me to the point where I thought: *I want to do more of this.* I love doing this work, because I think others feel the love and passion. It comes through me without work. It's natural, part of that authentic place in me.

Audrey Ellis Pyon

*"I not only believe that I'm worthy of love, I believe
that I am an expression of love…that we all are."*

Audrey Ellis Pyon is a Spiritual Relationship Mentor & Coach. Audrey
operates her coaching practice, In Joy Being, and is the author of the *In
Joy Being* blog. She works with her husband, Dr. Sammy Pyon, in their
El Segundo, California office. The Pyons' shared vision is "to create an
Evolutionary Healing Experience for every one they touch."

Audrey received her Master of Arts in Spiritual Psychology from the
University of Santa Monica. Prior to becoming a Spiritual Relationship
Coach and Mentor, she spent 15 years in the corporate world in Sales
& Customer Relationship Management working for companies such
as Ticketmaster-CitySearch and NationsBank, N.A. (now Bank of
America). She earned her MBA through Cal State and her BSBA
in Marketing from East Carolina University.   She lives in Southern
California with her husband and two children.

To find out more: (310) 322-1757 & audrey.injoybeing@gmail.com

**What personal event or universal problem made you want to do
what you do?**

I have been on a lifelong quest to figure out: *Why am I here?* Perhaps it
started with some early tragedy in my life, like my parents' divorce and
the transition from being "Daddy's Little Girl" to a relationship that felt
more like my father and I were acquaintances. A few years later, when I
was almost ten, my brother, David, passed away. He was just a month
shy of his twentieth birthday. David had filled the gap my father had left,

and he was the most important person in my life, next to my mom, at that time. That loss, combined with the loss of my father, started me on a quest to know: *Why am I here?* For years, I asked myself that question, along with others, such as: *Why was David taken and not me? What does that mean for me? What is this thing called "life" all about?*

I spent my life searching for meaning in my brother's death. What I realized was that the meaning was found in his life, and in the relationship we shared, not in his death. I found, ultimately, that my mission and purpose in this world is to be with others in witnessing, supporting, and empowering them to live and be in love and joy, which I believe is a universal need right now.

What I have discovered in my search, ultimately, is my faith: I believe that God is love. I am an expression of God's love; we *all* are expressions of God's love. I am here to spread the word of God (which to me *is* love), and so I go forward expressing loving-consciousness into the world as best I can today.

With that as my faith, my philosophy, and my truth, I've discovered that the best way for me to be in this world is to be in service and in support of others reconnecting with their authentic selves, their Sources, and their purposes, and inspiring and empowering them to reflect this into their worlds.

What has been the hardest part of doing what you do?

The things that are most challenging are also the most fulfilling and rewarding.

I've narrowed this down to two things. The first one is witnessing and being with others in their pain, whether it is the loss of a loved one, self-hatred that has run so deeply into them that they aren't sure of who they are anymore, or those who are seeking their purpose. One of the hardest things to do is simply to be with them in their pain, without trying to fix it or solve it for them, but just to be a supportive ear. At the same time, one of the most rewarding things is to be given the opportunity to be with someone in that pain and create a space of unconditional loving, compassion, trust, and authenticity for them to express freely their experience and to let them know they are not alone. In this space, I believe we discover our own answers.

That leads me to the second most challenging aspect, which is the reflection—the mirror—each client offers me to grow, to change, or to shift in my own world and in my own life. One of the most challenging aspects of what I do is being with people in pain and facing my own limitations in the reflection of the challenges that they face. This is also the most rewarding because there's something genuinely, deeply connected in being with another in this way and then learning and growing from it within my own life so I become better for everyone I touch.

What keeps you going when things are tough?

As a spiritual relationship coach, I doubt my answer to this question comes as a surprise. My relationships are what keep me going. The relationship, the connection, and intimacy I have with my husband, Sammy, brings me so much love and joy. He is the love of my life and my best friend. His faith and belief in me inspire, empower, and uplift me. Sammy is my closest mirror and our relationship has taught me so much about myself and what it means to be in relationship with someone. Our children, David and Sarah, teach me more than I will ever teach them, and their hugs make anything better. My family and friends surround me with so much love and support. I feel that my glass is neither half empty nor half full; it "runneth over." Without that, without those relationships, without that knowledge of love everywhere, I don't know how I would do it. I'm surrounded, in my darkest moments and throughout my life, with love and loving beings, and they remind me of who I am and empower me to keep going.

What's been the most rewarding part of what you do?

I mentioned some of those rewards already, but I think perhaps the greatest reward is to witness others remembering the loving beings they are...to witness them seeing the value of who they are, the value they create in their world, and that they make a difference in the lives of everyone they touch...witnessing the transformation of people who don't necessarily know their worth—who are hurting and have been in a space of self-doubt, fear, and worry for so long—and who begin to see the loving beings they are, the truth of the compassion they offer, and the beautiful gift of themselves in the world. I don't know how to truly describe that transformation, but I guess the closest thing is watching the dawn break, where light begins to make its way into the sky, the air is fresh and new, and it's quiet, and the world is just beginning to come alive...the glistening of a new morning, the freshness, the awakening, the light of it...it's like that. It's like the birth of a new day or maybe even the birth of a remembered being.

What is the most inspiring transformation or manifestation that you've witnessed in your work?

Every transformation I have been blessed to witness has been inspiring, and every manifestation reminds me of our beautiful ability to create, yet there is only one story that is mine to tell and that is my own.

After my brother's death and my parents' divorce, somewhere inside I began to tell myself that I was not worthy of love because my father had left, and that if I loved a man he would leave me, either by choice or by death. This did not bode well for me in the dating scene, let me tell you. I spent years making choices that gave me the evidence I needed to declare the above stories as true.

Yet here I am now, in a conscious, loving relationship with a man who inspires and empowers me, and whom I aspire to be more like. My family and friends fill my life with love, and my work is my love made visible. Best of all, I not only believe that I'm worthy of love, I believe that I am an expression of love…that we *all* are.

John Rozenberg

"Seeing people expand and grow and go beyond what they imagined as their own limitations, that's the most rewarding part of what I do."

John Rozenberg is an intuitive healer who provides private and group healing sessions, life coaching, and mentoring in the practical application of the Universal Law of Attraction, new paradigm business, and conscious life creation.

John leads workshops and retreats covering subjects ranging from cleansing and healing, to prosperity consciousness and sustainable living. John's life's work is to empower people to define, create, and live the life of their dreams.

To find out more: www.JohnRozenberg.com or (323) 363-5761

What personal event or universal problem made you want to do what you do?

There are so many people moving through life unconsciously. They do what they do without even knowing why they're doing it—from the most basic things, like waking up and going to an unfulfilling job, day after day, or staying in relationships that don't support their growth, to living in fear of, or hate for, people and things they've never even met or simply don't understand. These behaviors are all predicated on old beliefs and most of the time we don't even know where these beliefs came from. I work to bring awareness to peoples lives, to remind them that we each have a choice about what we do, and why and how we do it.

As for my personal event, in 2001 I had an experience that woke me up and really got my attention. I was sitting in a ballroom with about 100 other people, mostly strangers, during a weekend workshop. I looked across the room and made eye contact with one of these strangers, and I heard a very loud voice in my head say: *Healer*. At that moment, everything in my life suddenly made sense. Images of people, places, and events in my life flashed in my mind. It was like watching a high-speed slideshow of my life. All of these seemingly unrelated events suddenly became one long chain of teachings with a clear and definite purpose. I realized, in that moment, that I had been a healer my whole life; I just hadn't realized it.

I didn't share what I had experienced with anyone. As blown away as I was, I did my best to dismiss it.

Later that day, a man—another stranger—walked up to me and said, "I have a chronic back problem and you can fix it."

We had a brief conversation, I put my hand on his back, and I could feel his pain. I don't remember what we talked about, but 10 minutes later his pain was gone. How he recognized me as a healer, I don't know, but people have been showing up in this way ever since.

What has been the hardest part of doing what you do?

The hardest part has been looking at, and digging into, my own "stuff." I realize that to do this work with anyone else, I first have to do the work myself. Inevitably, when I'm going through something in my own life, the clients who show up are dealing with similar issues. I often have messages come through for them that are also exactly what I needed to hear in the moment.

We all have stuff to work through. I believe that transformation, or, as some would like to call it, "enlightenment," is an ongoing process. It's not a destination; it's something that we really need to be diligent about. We have to stay aware because just when we think we have all the answers, we find a whole new list of questions. I think that is what this process—our learning and making a difference—is really all about; it starts with checking ourselves first and asking honest questions.

What keeps you going when things are tough?

What keeps me going is knowing that things are never tough. Things simply are what they are. If they seem to be tough, it's just my perception of them at that moment and I'm probably getting in my own way somehow. When I step away from the situation for a minute and allow myself to get a new perspective, I realize things really aren't as tough as they seemed to be. What seems to be tough is just me not liking the situation, or maybe not getting the message in it. So, reminding myself that it just is what it is and I'm the one making it tough, and knowing *this too shall pass*, helps me get through.

What's been the most rewarding part of what you do?

The look on a client's face when they have that "aha" moment, that moment when they realize they *do* have a choice and they can choose anything they want…seeing a client, or anyone for that matter, fulfill their dreams and go beyond what they had dreamed…seeing someone push past their fears into a place of love is really rewarding. Some of my clients have posted testimonials on my website. I have never been able to read them all because I get so moved by what people say. It's very humbling. Seeing people expand and grow and go beyond what they imagined as their own limitations, that's the most rewarding part of what I do.

What is the most inspiring transformation or manifestation that you've witnessed in your work?

This is the hardest question to answer because I've seen so many. I've seen relationships that were broken for decades get resolved. I've worked with couples, in marriages that weren't working anymore, who have been healed. Whether they stayed together or separated as friends, they just came to a place of knowing that, at the core, there was a deep love and it was okay to move past whatever pain might be there. I've seen physical transformations, like one client who fulfilled her dream of running a marathon when she'd had trouble walking a short time earlier. I've seen so many of these transformations that it's really impossible to pick just one as the "most inspiring." My own transformation, over the years, has been dramatic to the point of me looking in the mirror one day and saying to myself: *Wow, who's that guy?* It's hard to put any one at the top of the list. I'd have to say that transformation is ongoing and just when I think I've seen the most amazing one, I'm blown away by another.

Maura Leon

"It's important to me that I don't allow my personal issues to get in the way of my commitment to the people I serve."

Maura Leon is an inspirational publisher and author, intuitive life coach, and vibrational artist. Her Vibrational Visioning process has been praised by transformational leaders, including best-selling authors Marci Shimoff and Maribel Jimenez.

Over ten years ago, Maura succeeded in manifesting the relationship of her dreams, using a specific process to attract exactly what she wanted. She then discovered that her soul mate, Keith, had used the exact same process to attract her. Realizing that they had a common mission, Keith and Maura wrote and published their first book, *The Seven Steps to Successful Relationships*, and began teaching people how to communicate better, love themselves more completely, and make their dream lives a reality.

Maura has appeared on popular radio and television broadcasts, including "The Rolonda Watts Show" and "The Shelley Martin Show," and her work has been covered by newspapers such as *The Minneapolis–St. Paul Star Tribune* and *The Maryland Herald-Mail*. Maura's articles have been featured in *Succeed Magazine* and *The Huffington Post*, and she is a featured teacher in the upcoming film, *The Gratitude Experiment*.

Maura has spoken at events that included T. Harv Eker, Marianne Williamson, Brian Tracy, Marcia Martin, Bob Doyle, Jennifer McLean, Keith Leon, and Maribel Jimenez. Her passion is taking transformational leaders to their next level.

To find out more: www.MauraLeon.com

What personal event or universal problem made you want to do what you do?

That's an interesting question, because a personal event and a universal problem can be two separate things, or they can be very connected. I've found that when I focus on my own personal issues, which I tended to do a lot when I was younger, my life is just a mess and doesn't work well at all. When I focus on someone else's struggles, and how I can be there for them in a caring and compassionate way, while still taking care of myself, things always seem to work out better in my life.

Universally, what I saw, growing up, was that we humans, as a species, don't seem to choose systems that work well for us, and it was very frustrating for me, because nobody else seemed to notice this at all. Our systems of government and finance seemed particularly dysfunctional to me and, for a while, I thought that my path was going to involve opting out of mainstream society and joining an intentional community. While I never found one that felt like a fit for me, I did, eventually, discover that there were like-minded people out there who were sharing their wisdom and experience in a way that truly resonated with me. The first one I remember being introduced to was Marianne Williamson; I received a copy of the audio version of her book, *A Return to Love*, and I listened to it over and over, because it made more sense to me than anything I had experienced up to that point. My internal guidance system gave me a big, giant *YES* to that book, and it seemed like everything I had experienced before that had been a big, giant *NO*.

I also resonated, deeply, with Richard Bach's *Illusions*, Ruth Ross' *Prospering Woman*, and Louise Hay's *You Can Heal Your Life*. These authors were all presenting possible solutions to the universal problems I was seeing in society, and while it was wonderful to feel such a powerful connection to mentors who spoke to my heart in such a profound way, I was longing to feel a similar connection to my peers; I wanted to experience a deeper level of compassion, innovation, and inspiration with the people in my life.

What I now understand is that once you start on the path of self-growth, even if it's just by having a new kind of conversation or reading a new kind of book, your path will continue to unfold in front of you; the way will always be shown. The beautiful way that I was shown was through the dynamic world of personal development seminars. I attended my first Insight Seminar in the fall of 1996 and, by the time it was over, I knew I was home. At the end of the follow-up event, I stuck around to help clean up, but that was just an excuse. I didn't want to leave. I was so comfortable there—actually, no—"comfortable" is not the right word, because I was nervous as heck! "Compelled" is more like it. The leader of the event had already left, and I found myself walking up to the front of the room and sitting down in his chair, just to see what it felt like. One of the team leaders saw me and gave me a knowing look, saying, "Mm-hmm…now, you remember that." (I think he must have previously experienced exactly what I was feeling at that moment.)

So, that was it for me. I knew I had found who I really was and what I wanted to do with my life. It felt more right than anything ever had, so I kept going, and within a little over a year, I had taken all of the basic and advanced courses that the organization offered. They called me a "fast-tracker" and I definitely was one. When I got into their Leadership program and had an opportunity to identify my top life goals, I realized that my number one goal was to have the relationship of my dreams, so I embraced the process of manifesting that relationship. Guess what… it worked! Not only did I attract a man, but I found out that the man I attracted had done the exact same process, and we were an amazingly perfect match. We decided to write a book about how we did it, so we could inspire others to do the same thing. Once again, my path was unfolding before me and I had now come full circle, from being inspired by transformational authors, to becoming one myself.

By the time I discovered life coaching, as a profession, I was already an entrepreneur, a publisher, an author, and a speaker, so I was able to attract coaching clients who were a perfect match, because they resonated with what I teach. I absolutely love what I do, and it just keeps getting better and better.

What has been the hardest part of doing what you do?

Actually, the hardest part is finding enough time to do all the things I want to do. I am constantly downloading great ideas and I don't have the time to implement all of them. Originally, I thought it was an issue of life balance but since that's one of the main subjects that I coach in, I've had the opportunity to learn as much about that as I had already learned about relationships and the Law of Attraction. It's an ongoing process of discovery, but I would say that, just as it is with most people, the thing that most gets in my way is me. When I let go of that and focus on others, then everything flows. Especially when I can be in the moment, be present, stop worrying, and just trust.

What keeps you going when things are tough?

My inner vision and my passion keep me going, and it also helps to remember my victories, both large and small. The more experiences I've accumulated of things going well, the easier it becomes, in the darker moments, to trust that it's going to work out, and that, not only is it going to work out, it's going to be awesome! So I keep my focus on that.

The other thing that keeps me going is the people I'm committed to. In my drive for success, I set myself up into a situation in which I now have a responsibility to be accountable to a large number of people, not just to myself. It's important to me that I don't allow my personal issues to get in the way of my commitment to the people I serve. I now know—because I've proved it more than once—that I can be there for myself and be there for others as well. That was something I really wanted to learn how to do, because I am naturally a caretaker and it had taken its toll on me for a long time. Now I don't have to sacrifice my well-being for others, so I don't have to be selfish in that way anymore. I learned that if I let go of resistance and embrace, with love and gratitude, whatever is present in each moment, and then make my decisions from that place of inner peace, I receive all that I need for myself—perfect energy, perfect love, perfect health, perfect financial flow—and I can tap into the unlimited Source of all things and give freely to others.

One of the people who continually teaches me this lesson is Keith Leon. As my husband, my best friend, and my business partner, Keith is my day in/day out accountability buddy, and I am happy to be the same for him. We hold each other to an even higher standard than each of us holds for ourselves. We remind each other who we really are. It's such a blessing in my life. I couldn't ask for a better support system.

What's been the most rewarding part of what you do?

I think the most rewarding thing is seeing the growth in myself and in the people I work with. It feels so good when I see how I've changed for the better. It's so rewarding to see others benefiting from what I do, when what I do comes so naturally to me and I love it so much. Seeing myself, and other people, healing from mental, emotional, and physical conditions, healing relationships, and shifting financial conditions is incredibly satisfying. It's mind-blowing because mainstream conditioning and society would try to tell us that we couldn't do it. My husband always talks about how we live to prove the teachings of Jesus Christ, and I'm really starting to see how that's true. Not just Jesus, but the other prophets and spiritual leaders as well; they were all teaching the same thing. It's not about worshiping someone or something outside of me, it's about rediscovering, trusting, and activating the power within me. And in the moments when I'm aware of the potential of that power, within me, to make a difference in the world, there is nothing more rewarding than that.

What is the most inspiring transformation or manifestation that you've witnessed in your work?

I've seen many amazing transformations and manifestations. The ones that stand out most for me are the ones I've witnessed in the people closest to me.

The earliest transformation, which had a great impact on me, was my sister's recovery from a bone marrow transplant. That was a biggie. For that procedure, they basically give you enough chemo drugs to almost kill you, and then you just do whatever you can to bring yourself back to life and hope that it works. I was living with my sister at the time, so I was with her during her recovery period, after they sent her home from the hospital. I had never seen anybody that close to death before, and I really had no idea what to do to help her heal, but that didn't matter, because she knew exactly what to do. I think it was intuitive; she just knew. The main thing she did was make herself laugh. I've heard this from other people, too, who have survived similar situations. I am convinced that that is what brought her back to the excellent health she enjoys today. Her favorite thing was to read the books of the humor columnist, Dave Barry. I never knew just how hilarious he was until that experience. She would read them to herself, and she would also have me read them out loud to her, so we could both laugh together. What an awesome demonstration of the difference a book can make in someone's life. Thanks, Dave!

I witnessed many other transformations, in myself and others, over the years: my mother-in-law bringing herself back from death's door because she wasn't ready to go; my stepson's miraculously rapid and complete recovery from emergency brain surgery after a life-threatening head trauma; my husband's journey from obesity to vibrant health; our business making it through the severe economic downturn to not only survive, but thrive; and my own healing journey from an "incurable disease" to the healthiest I've ever been. I can't tell you how gratifying it is to realize that every one of these transformations was affected by me in some way. My love and support made a difference. My trust, in myself and in the process of life, made a difference. My steady vision and unwavering commitment made a difference. I am profoundly grateful, and I know that as long as I continue to believe that I can make a difference...I will.

Barbara De Angelis

"There's nothing more profound than offering people ways to experience more freedom and mastery in their lives."

Barbara De Angelis, Ph.D. is one of the most influential teachers of our time in the field of relationships and personal growth. For the past twenty-five years, she has reached tens of millions of people throughout the world with her positive messages about love, happiness, and the search for meaning in our lives. As a best-selling author, popular television personality, and sought-after motivational speaker, Barbara has been a pioneer in the field of personal transformation as one of the first people to popularize the idea of self-help in the 1980s, and as one of the first nationally recognized female motivational teachers on television.

Barbara is the author of 14 best-selling books which have sold over eight million copies and been published throughout the world in twenty languages. Titles include *How to Make Love All the Time, Chicken Soup for the Romantic Soul, Chicken Soup for the Couples Soul,* and *Secrets about Life Every Woman Should Know.* Barbara has written regularly for magazines including *Cosmopolitan, Ladies Home Journal, McCall's, Readers Digest, Redbook,* and *Family Circle.* Barbara's latest book is *How Did I Get Here? Finding Your Way to Renewed Hope and Happiness When Life and Love Take Unexpected Turns.*

Barbara's television career has been just as prolific as her publishing career. She has been a frequent guest on "Oprah," "The Today Show," "Good Morning America," "The View," "Geraldo," and "Politically Incorrect," as well as a regular contributor to "E Entertainment" and "Eyewitness News" in Los Angeles. Barbara also produced and starred in a one hour special for PBS entitled "Love Secrets."

Over the past twenty years, Barbara has been in demand as a motivational speaker in North America, giving hundreds of presentations to groups including AT&T, Proctor & Gamble, Crystal Cruise Lines, and Young Presidents' Organization.

To find out more: www.BarbaraDeAngelis.com

What personal event or universal problem made you want to do what you do?

I don't think it was an event or anything that came from my mind, or a plan, or the idea of wanting to make a difference, from an intellectual point of view. It was really a soul calling—something I felt, from the time I was very young, that I was *supposed* to do. It was not something that I wanted—or didn't want—to do, or needed to do, but that I was supposed to do. I was here for a reason. When I looked around, I saw the need for more consciousness on the planet. The more I grew and understood what that meant—in whatever way, at the time in my career, I felt I could bring more light—that's what I've always done. It was really an assignment, the way I look at it...something I agreed to do before I came here. I was just fulfilling that promise.

What has been the hardest part of doing what you do?

There is loneliness in being a spiritual teacher. There is a trajectory of experience working with people at the deepest level...holding steady in the faith of the darkness of the planet, and having access to so much wisdom, inspiration, and cosmic energy that flows through. That creates a certain kind of separation, even in the midst of tremendous universal love and connection. That's something that, as I've grown over the decades, I have had to face, as I once studied and read many spiritual teachers do. The other piece of that is...when I can see more for people than they can see for themselves...when I can love people more than they can feel love for themselves...when I care more about somebody's freedom than they do for themselves...that is painful. Learning to know the difference between when somebody is really ready to shift and when they're not has been a very important lesson for me as a teacher. I always say, there's a difference between trying to give people things, and offering. You can offer a meal, but you can't stuff it down people's throats. The ego has to get out of the way completely, and one has to offer with love and compassion, and be unattached, in a sense, to whether or not that delicious meal is received or appreciated. These are things that have been great lessons for me to learn.

What keeps you going when things are tough?

The resonance of the truth inside of me is like a sanctuary I can always retreat back to. My own movement towards freedom, and the tremendous gifts that it offers, has been the thing that has always given me great courage to do this work. Since it's coming from my own experience, my own journey, and not from the *desire* to help people but from the *knowingness* of what's possible, that knowingness gives me tremendous strength, dedication, and commitment to share the path I've traveled— and ways to travel it more easily—with others.

The other thing that has always kept me going is the same answer to the first question: the feeling that it's not a choice for me. It's not an option; it's an assignment. It would be like saying to a mother, "What keeps you going in parenting your child?" because I'm the mother. So, for me, this is what I'm supposed to do. Whether it's ecstatic one day…difficult another day…it's what I'm supposed to do. Knowing that, and knowing that that's a privilege, is what continues to sustain me.

What's been the most rewarding part of what you do?

There's nothing more profound than offering people ways to experience more freedom and mastery in their lives. At this point, there are, literally, millions of people I've helped through my books, seminars, and television shows; it's a very humbling thought, and a very, very gratifying thought. Every day I receive emails, letters, and phone calls—and I have for a long time—from people all over the world, thanking me for ways that I've made a difference, or telling me that a book has made a difference…a *huge* difference. I know that I'm not even aware of how much of a difference I've made, like most of us aren't. It's those people, who have become more illuminated from my work and what's come through me, who give me the strength to go out and keep offering to people I don't know yet. So, in a sense, even my students or my readers are helping to pass along the wisdom, the message, and the love, by loving me back and mirroring back to me what effect I've had on them. That, then, expands out to the next group waiting.

What is the most inspiring transformation or manifestation that you've witnessed in your work?

I can't choose one thing. It's not a story of, "There was this one person who had this horrible thing, and then this happened." I have thousands and thousands and thousands of stories like that. I think, for me, it's not particularly about a moment, but about the potential in the moment… when, for instance, I'll have a large group of people who have just come to take a seminar with me, and I can do something in five minutes that pulls all of them into their highest, allows them to see the highest light within each other, and, in five minutes, the room feels like Heaven and people are having an experience of love they didn't think was possible. It's the manifestation of the shift people can make, so quickly…the connection people can make to their highest, so quickly, without realizing they have that ability. The impact that has on hundreds of people around them that, to me, is awe-inspiring. I know that that's possible, I know how to help facilitate that, and every time I do (which is all the time), I am equally amazed at the potential we all have, as human beings, to create our own joy or sorrow, Heaven or Hell, or freedom or bondage, in each moment. *That's* a miracle, and it's not one miracle I've seen, but it's a *continuous* miracle. I feel very privileged to be part of creating the space for that miracle to occur.